Apache Solr PHP Integration

Build a fully-featured and scalable search application
using PHP to unlock the search functions provided
by Solr

Jayant Kumar

PUBLISHING

BIRMINGHAM - MUMBAI

Apache Solr PHP Integration

First published: November 2013

Production Reference: 1181113

Published by Packt Publishing Ltd.
Livery Place
35 Livery Street
Birmingham B3 2PB, UK.

ISBN 978-1-78216-492-0

www.packtpub.com

Cover Image by Aniket Sawant (aniket_sawant_photography@hotmail.com)

Credits

Author
Jayant Kumar

Reviewers
Renoir Boulanger
Ruben Teijeiro

Acquisition Editor
Luke Presland

Commisioning Editor
Amit Ghodake

Technical Editors
Sharvari H. Baet
Nadeem Bagban

Project Coordinator
Suraj Bist

Proofreader
Ting Baker

Indexer
Monica Ajmera Mehta

Production Coordinator
Melwyn D'sa

Cover Work
Melwyn D'sa

About the Author

Jayant Kumar is an experienced software professional and a Bachelor of Engineering in Computer Science, with more than 12 years' of experience in architecting and developing large-scale web applications.

Jayant is an expert on search technologies and PHP and has been working with Lucene and Solr for more than 10 years now. He has been the key person responsible for introducing Lucene as a search engine in www.naukri.com, the most successful job portal in India.

Jayant has played many different important roles throughout his career, including software developer, team leader, project manager, and architect, but his primary focus has been on building scalable solutions on the web. Currently, he is associated with the digital division of HT Media as the Chief Architect responsible for the job site www.shine.com.

Jayant is an avid blogger and his blog can be visited at http://jayant7k.blogspot.in. His LinkedIn profile is available at http://www.linkedin.com/in/jayantkumar.

I would like to thank the guys at Packt Publishing for giving me the opportunity to write this book. Special thanks to Yogesh, Suraj, and Amit for keeping me engaged and dealing with my drafts and providing feedback at all stages.

I would like to thank my wife Nidhi and my parents for taking care of our kids while I was engaged in writing the book. And finally, I would like to thank my kids, Ashlesha and Banhishikha, for bearing with me while I was writing this book.

About the Reviewers

Renoir Boulanger is an application developer fascinated with web standards. He has been developing websites and web applications in PHP for over 10 years. His experience includes server management and web development for several communications agencies in the province of Quebec. He has created web integration libraries, and participated in the development of various specialized web applications, some of which were for big-name clients such as the W3C, Ericsson, Telefilm Canada, and the Union des Artistes du Québec.

Renoir's involvement in the W3C is as a member of developer relations and system teams, mainly contributing to the WebPlatform Docs (http://webplatform.org/) project to maintain the site stability, improve the site features, strengthen the hosting, and deployment infrastructure, act as a technical liaison with open source communities, and contribute to the success of the site.

In addition to having an easily identifiable name on the web, he can be found as @renoirb or at https://renoirboulanger.com/#is.

Ruben Teijeiro is an experienced frontend and backend web developer and has worked with several PHP frameworks for over a decade. His expertise is focused now on Drupal with which he has collaborated in the development of several projects for important companies such as Unicef and Telefonica in Spain and Ericsson in Sweden.

As an active member of the Drupal community you can find him contributing to Drupal Core, helping and mentoring other contributors, and speaking at Drupal events around the world. He also loves to share what he has learned on his blog at http://drewpull.com.

> I would like to express my deepest gratitude to the Drupal community. Without your help this would not be possible. A special thanks to my parents for their help and support and lastly to my girlfriend, Ana, who pushes me to be a better person.

www.PacktPub.com

Support files, eBooks, discount offers, and more

You might want to visit www.PacktPub.com for support files and downloads related to your book.

Did you know that Packt offers eBook versions of every book published, with PDF and ePub files available? You can upgrade to the eBook version at www.PacktPub.com and as a print book customer, you are entitled to a discount on the eBook copy. Get in touch with us at service@packtpub.com for more details.

At www.PacktPub.com, you can also read a collection of free technical articles, sign up for a range of free newsletters and receive exclusive discounts and offers on Packt books and eBooks.

http://PacktLib.PacktPub.com

Do you need instant solutions to your IT questions? PacktLib is Packt's online digital book library. Here, you can access, read and search across Packt's entire library of books.

Why subscribe?

- Fully searchable across every book published by Packt
- Copy and paste, print and bookmark content
- On-demand and accessible via web browsers

Free access for Packt account holders

If you have an account with Packt at www.PacktPub.com, you can use this to access PacktLib today and view nine entirely free books. Simply use your login credentials for immediate access.

Table of Contents

Preface

Searches are an integral part of any web application that is built today. Whether it is a content site, a job site, an e-commerce site, or any other website, searches play a very important role in helping the user locate the information that he/she is looking for. As a developer, it is imperative to provide the user of the website with all the possible tools for searching and narrowing down to the required information. Apache Solr is a full text search engine, which provides a large list of features for searches. PHP is the preferred programming language for building websites. This book guides the reader on the integration between PHP and Solr.

When a user performs a search on the website, he wants the results to be relevant based on certain criteria. Let us take the example of an e-commerce website. A search can happen on product names, brand names, model numbers, and product types. Once the results are visible, it is important to provide a set of facets on price, size, and some other features of the products in the search result, which can be used to narrow down the results to exactly what is desired. Autocompleting the search query as the user types and providing spelling suggestions are some of the advanced search functionalities that are visible on some websites.

The idea of this book is to bring attention to these and many other search functionalities that Solr provides to the community of PHP developers and to guide PHP developers who build these websites on exploring and using these search functionalities to build features related to searches into their websites. This book not only provides a quick step-by-step PHP code for fast development of search features but also goes in depth on how the feature actually works on the Solr end. Configurations and tweaking options in Solr and PHP are also discussed for advanced users to help them tweak the functionality as per their requirements.

This book will start with installation of Solr, adding, updating, and deleting documents on Solr using PHP and then exploring the features provided by the Solr search. We will explore the features provided by Solr such as faceting, grouping, boosting, and sorting of results. We will build a spell check and a query autocomplete feature provided by Solr. We will also look at advanced features for scaling search. This book will provide an end-to-end practical guide to building a full featured search application using PHP and Solr.

What this book covers

Chapter 1, Installing and Integrating Solr and PHP, introduces Solr and installs and integrates Solr with PHP on both Windows and Linux environments.

Chapter 2, Inserting, Updating, and Deleting Documents from Solr, provides practical examples on how to use PHP to add, modify, and delete documents from the Solr index.

Chapter 3, Select Query on Solr and Query Modes (DisMax/eDisMax), explains how to run basic search queries on Solr and use different query modes to run some advanced search queries.

Chapter 4, Advanced Queries – Filter Queries and Faceting, digs deeper into search queries and provides practical examples for running filter queries and facets using Solr and PHP.

Chapter 5, Highlighting Results Using PHP and Solr, explains how Solr can be configured for highlighting search results and provides practical examples in PHP for highlighting.

Chapter 6, Debug and Stats Component, explains how Solr calculates relevance, ranks the results of a search query, and explains how index statistics can be obtained.

Chapter 7, Spell Check in Solr, configures Solr for spell check and provides practical example of an autocomplete feature built using PHP and Solr.

Chapter 8, Advanced Solr – Grouping, the MoreLikeThis Query, and Distributed Search, goes in depth on some of the advanced topics in Solr and also explains how Solr can be scaled horizontally.

What you need for this book

You will need a Windows or Linux machine with Apache Web Server configured to run PHP scripts. A file editor for writing code and a web browser to check the output of code execution will be needed. We will be downloading, installing, and configuring Solr as required.

Who this book is for

This book is for PHP developers who need to build and integrate search into their applications. No prior knowledge of Solr is required. Understanding of object oriented programming using PHP would be helpful. Readers should be familiar with the concept of web applications.

Conventions

In this book, you will find a number of styles of text that distinguish between different kinds of information. Here are some examples of these styles, and an explanation of their meaning.

Code words in the text are shown as follows: "Call the `createPing()` function to create the ping query."

A block of code is set as follows:

```
$config = array(
  "endpoint" => array("localhost" => array("host"=>"127.0.0.1",
"port"=>"8080", "path"=>"/solr", "core"=>"collection1",)
) );
```

Any command-line input or output is written as follows:

```
cd ~/solr-4.3.1/example
java -jar start.jar
```

New terms and *important words* are shown in italics. Words that you see on the screen, in menus or dialog boxes for example, appear in the text like this: "Select **collection1** from the dropdown on the left-hand panel. Click on **ping** and you will see the ping time in milliseconds appear next to the **ping** link".

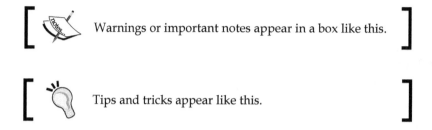

Warnings or important notes appear in a box like this.

Tips and tricks appear like this.

Reader feedback

Feedback from our readers is always welcome. Let us know what you think about this book—what you liked or may have disliked. Reader feedback is important for us to develop titles that you really get the most out of.

To send us general feedback, simply send an e-mail to feedback@packtpub.com, and mention the book title through the subject of your message.

If there is a topic that you have expertise in and you are interested in either writing or contributing to a book, see our author guide on www.packtpub.com/authors.

Customer support

Now that you are the proud owner of a Packt book, we have a number of things to help you to get the most from your purchase.

Downloading the example code

You can download the example code files for all Packt books you have purchased from your account at http://www.packtpub.com. If you purchased this book elsewhere, you can visit http://www.packtpub.com/support and register to have the files e-mailed directly to you.

Errata

Although we have taken every care to ensure the accuracy of our content, mistakes do happen. If you find a mistake in one of our books—maybe a mistake in the text or the code—we would be grateful if you would report this to us. By doing so, you can save other readers from frustration and help us improve subsequent versions of this book. If you find any errata, please report them by visiting http://www.packtpub.com/support, selecting your book, clicking on the **errata submission form** link, and entering the details of your errata. Once your errata are verified, your submission will be accepted and the errata will be uploaded to our website, or added to any list of existing errata, under the Errata section of that title.

Piracy

Piracy of copyright material on the Internet is an ongoing problem across all media. At Packt, we take the protection of our copyright and licenses very seriously. If you come across any illegal copies of our works, in any form, on the Internet, please provide us with the location address or website name immediately so that we can pursue a remedy.

Please contact us at copyright@packtpub.com with a link to the suspected pirated material.

We appreciate your help in protecting our authors, and our ability to bring you valuable content.

Questions

You can contact us at questions@packtpub.com if you are having a problem with any aspect of the book, and we will do our best to address it.

1
Installing and Integrating Solr and PHP

Are you a PHP programmer? Do you feel the need to incorporate search in your applications? Are you aware of Apache Solr? Do you feel it is a very tedious job to integrate Solr into your PHP applications? This book will make the integration easy for you. We will be looking at an end-to-end integration of Apache Solr with PHP. We will start with Solr installation. We will look at how Solr can be integrated with PHP. We will then explore the features provided by Solr through PHP code. After going through the book, you should be able to integrate almost all features provided by Solr into your PHP applications.

This chapter will help us in installing Apache Solr in two major environments: Windows and Linux. We will also go ahead and explore installation of Solr as part of Apache Tomcat Server. We will discuss the options available for talking to Solr via PHP and also learn how to set up the Solarium library for Solr PHP integration.

We will be covering the following topics in this chapter:

- What is Solr?
- Downloading and installing Solr on Windows and Linux
- Configuring Tomcat to run Solr.
- Executing ping queries on Solr using PHP
- Discussing different libraries for Solr PHP integration
- Installing Solarium on Windows and Linux
- Connecting PHP to Solr using Solarium
- Running ping queries using PHP and Solarium
- Checking Solr logs

Solr

You are PHP programmers and you build websites such as a job site, an e-commerce website, a content website, or others. You need to provide a search box for searching either jobs or products or other content in your website. How do you go about it? Do you do a "like" search in your database or probably use the full-text search available in MySQL—if you are using MySQL. Would you prefer to use some other platform that does the search for you and also provides you a huge set of features to tune the search as per your requirements?

Solr is an open source Java application providing an interface to the full-text search library known as Lucene. Both Solr and Lucene are a part of the Apache Lucene project. Apache Solr uses Apache Lucene as its core for search. Apache Lucene is an open source search API built in Java. In addition to full-text search, Solr also provides a huge set of features such as hit highlighting and faceted search.

Installing Solr

Solr requires the presence of Java on your system. To check the presence of Java on your system, run java -version in Linux console or Windows command prompt. If the version of Java is greater than 1.6 then we are ready to go. It is preferable to use the official Java Runtime Environment rather than the one provided by OpenJDK.

```
c:\>java -version
java version "1.6.0_18"
Java(TM) SE Runtime Environment (build 1.6.0_18-b07)
Java HotSpot(TM) Client VM (build 16.0-b13, mixed mode, sharing)
```

Let us download the latest Solr. For this book we are using Solr Version 4.3.1, which can be downloaded from the following link:

http://lucene.apache.org/solr/downloads.html

To install Solr on Windows or Linux simply unzip or extract the solr-4.3.1.zip file into a folder. The installation process for Windows and Linux is as follows:

- For installation on Windows, simply right-click on the zip file and extract it into the C:\solr-4.3.1 folder. To start Solr, go to the Windows command prompt **Start | Run**. In the **Run** window, type cmd. On the Windows command prompt type the following:

    ```
    cd C:\solr-4.3.1\example
    java -jar start.jar
    ```

- For installation on Linux, simply extract the zip file in your home folder. Follow these commands to extract and run Solr using your console:

```
unzip solr-4.3.1.zip
cd ~/solr-4.3.1/example
java -jar start.jar
```

When we start Solr with the `java -jar start.jar` option, Solr runs on the port 8983. It uses a built-in web server known as jetty. To see Solr working, simply point your browser to the following address:

```
http://localhost:8983/solr/
```

You will be able to see the following interface. This means that Solr is running fine. The following screenshot shows the **Solr Admin** interface:

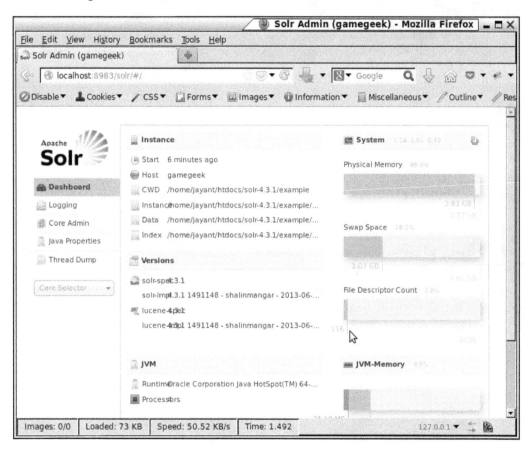

Configuring Tomcat to run Solr

The web server jetty used by default Solr is meant for development purposes only. For production environment, we would want Solr to run as a part of a more convenient setup involving a more reliable web server. Solr can be configured to run on any J2EE container such as IBM Websphere or JBoss or any other server. Apache Tomcat is the most commonly used server. Let us see how to set up Solr as a part of Apache Tomcat web server. We have Apache Tomcat installed on our Windows or Linux environment.

To run Solr as a part of Apache Tomcat web server, you need to create a context for /solr in the configuration. The following solr.xml file needs to be put at the appropriate location in Windows and Linux inside the Tomcat configuration folder at <tomcat_home>/conf/Catalina/localhost.

```
<?xml version="1.0" encoding="UTF-8"?>
<Context docBase="/home/jayant/solr-4.3.1/example/webapps/solr.war" >
<Environment name="solr/home" type="java.lang.String" value="/home/
jayant/solr-4.3.1/example/solr" override="true" />
</Context>
```

Change docBase to <solr_path>/example/webapps/solr.war and the value attribute in Environment to <solr_path>/example/solr. The environment named solr/home tells Tomcat the location where Solr configuration files are to be found. In addition to this, let us change the configuration of Solr in the <solr_path>/example/solr/solr.xml file. Search for hostPort and change it to match Tomcat's port 8080. Similarly search for hostContext and change it to solr.

 Windows users, use \ instead of / in your configuration XML files for path variables. Do not change the / in solr/home.

Restart your Tomcat server and you should be able to go to the following URL to see Solr working along with Tomcat:

```
http://localhost:8080/solr/
```

If you see an error "404 not found" on the preceding URL, it may be because of some libraries of Solr that Tomcat is not able to find. You can check the exact error in Tomcat error logs in the `<tomcat_home>/logs/catalina.out` folder. To resolve the missing library issue, copy all JAR files from the `<solr_home>/example/lib/ext` to `<tomcat_home>/lib` folder.

You can also enable advanced logging in your Tomcat logs by copying the `log4j.properties` file from the `<solr_home>/example/resources` folder to your `<tomcat_home>/lib` folder.

Executing a ping query on Solr using PHP

Ping queries are used in Solr to monitor the health of the Solr server. Let us first see how the ping query works on the **Solr Admin** web interface:

1. Open up the browser and go to the URL for Solr.

2. Select **collection1** from the dropdown on the left-hand side panel.

3. Click on **Ping** and you will see the ping time in milliseconds appear next to the ping's link. Our ping is working fine.

Let us check the version of PHP installed. We need Version 5.3.2 and above. To check the version, run `php -v` on the Windows or Linux command line as follows:

```
c:\>php -v
PHP 5.4.16 (cli) (built: Jun  5 2013 21:01:46)
Copyright (c) 1997-2013 The PHP Group
Zend Engine v2.4.0, Copyright (c) 1998-2013 Zend Technologies
```

To get ping working from our PHP code, we will need a utility called cURL. For Linux environments, we need to install the `curl`, `libcurl`, and `php5-curl` packages. On Ubuntu distribution of Linux it can be installed using the following command:

```
sudo apt-get install curl php5-curl
```

For enabling cURL on windows, we need to edit the `php.ini` file in our PHP installation. Search for the extensions directory setting and change it to where `php_curl.dll` is located. Also, uncomment the line which loads `php_curl.dll`:

```
extension=php_curl.dll
extension_dir = "C:\php\ext"
```

The following URL is the URL that is being called for executing the ping query. On going to this URL, we can see the response that contains the response header and the status, which is OK.

```
http://localhost:8080/solr/collection1/admin/ping
```

We can see that the response is in XML. To convert the response to JSON, simply add `wt=json` to the earlier URL:

```
http://localhost:8080/solr/collection1/admin/ping/?wt=json
```

Linux users can check the response of a curl call using the following command:

```
curl http://localhost:8080/solr/collection1/admin/ping/?wt=json
{"responseHeader":{"status":0,"QTime":7,"params":{"df":"text","echoParams":"all","rows":"10","echoParams":"all","wt":"json","q":"solrpingquery","distrib":"false"}},"status":"OK"}
```

A direct call to Solr via PHP requires us to call the ping with a JSON response URL via cURL and decode the JSON response to show the result. Here is a piece of code to do the same. This code can be executed using the PHP command line:

```
$curl = curl_init("http://localhost:8080/solr/collection1/admin/
ping/?wt=json");
curl_setopt($curl, CURLOPT_RETURNTRANSFER, 1);
$output = curl_exec($curl);
```

```
$data = json_decode($output, true);
echo "Ping Status : ".$data["status"]."\n";
```

On executing the preceding code via command line, we will get the output as follows:

```
Ping Status : OK
```

Downloading the example code

You can download the example code files for all Packt books you have purchased from your account at http://www.PacktPub.com. If you purchased this book elsewhere, you can visit http://www.PacktPub.com/support and register to have the files e-mailed directly to you.

Libraries available for PHP-Solr integration

Every call to Solr for executing any task is eventually a URL which needs particular parameters depending on what we need to get done. So, adding documents to Solr, deleting documents from Solr, and searching of documents can all be done by building URLs with parameters for their respective commands. We can call these URLs using PHP and cURL and interpret the response in JSON. However, instead of remembering every command to be sent in the URL, we can use a library to create the Solr URL and interpret the response. Some of the libraries available are as follows:

- Solr-PHP-client
- Apache Solr-PHP extension
- Solarium

Solr-PHP-client can be obtained from the following location:

```
https://code.google.com/p/solr-php-client/
```

It can be seen that the latest release for this library was in November 2009. There have been no developments on this library since 2009. This is a very basic client and does not support a lot of features that are now available in Solr.

Apache SolrPhp extension can be obtained from the following location:

```
http://pecl.php.net/package/solr
```

The latest release for this library was in November 2011. This is a comparatively better library. And is also the library suggested for integrating with Solr on www.php.net. It is intended to be very fast and lightweight compared to others. The complete API of the library can be obtained from following location:

```
http://php.net/manual/en/book.solr.php
```

Solarium is the latest library for Solr PHP integration. It is open source and is continuously updated. It is fully object oriented and provides features almost as soon as they are made available in Solr. It is fully flexible where you can add a functionality that you feel is missing. Also custom parameters can be used to achieve almost any task. On the downside, the library is somewhat heavy as it has many files. Solarium replicates the concepts of Solr to some extent. And it is being actively developed. We will install Solarium and explore the comprehensive list of features of Solr via PHP code using the Solarium library.

Installing Solarium

Solarium can be downloaded and used directly or it can be installed using a package manager for PHP called Composer. If we download the Solarium library directly, we will have to get other dependencies for installation. Composer, on the other hand, manages all dependencies by itself. Let us have a quick look at installing Composer on both Windows and Linux environments.

For Linux, the following commands will help in installation of Composer:

```
curl https://getcomposer.org/installer | php
mv composer.phar composer
```

These command downloads the Composer installer PHP script and passes the output to the PHP program for interpretation and execution. During execution, the PHP script downloads the Composer code into a single executable PHP program composer.phar (PHP Archive). We are renaming the composer.phar executable to Composer for ease of use purposes. On Linux, Composer can be installed at a user level or at a global level. To install Composer at user level, simply add it to your environment path using the following command:

```
export PATH=<path to composer>:$PATH
```

To install Composer on a global level simply move it to the system path such as /usr/bin or /usr/local/bin. To check if Composer has been installed successfully, simply run Composer on your console and check the various options provided by Composer.

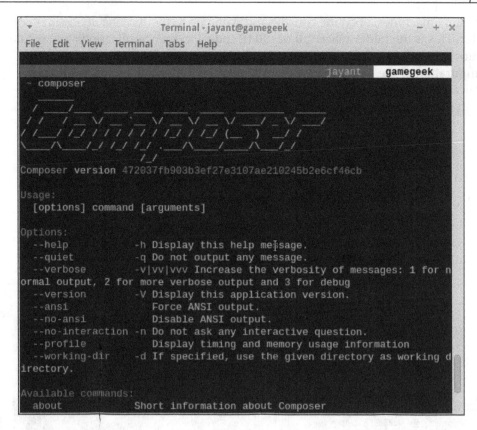

Windows user can download `composer-setup.exe` from the following link:

`http://getcomposer.org/Composer-Setup.exe`

Double-click on the executable and follow instructions to install Composer.

We will need to install a web server—mostly Apache and configure it to enable the execution of PHP scripts on it.

Alternatively, we can use the built-in web server in PHP 5.4. This server can be started by going to the directory where all HTML and PHP files are and by using the `php -S localhost:8000` command to start the PHP development server on port 8000 on our local machine.

Once Composer is in place, installing Solarium is pretty easy. Let us install Solarium on both Linux and Windows machine.

For Linux machines, open the console and navigate to the Apache documentRoot folder. This is the folder where all our PHP code and web applications will reside. In most cases, it is /var/www or it can be changed to any folder by changing the configuration of the web server. Create a separate folder where you want your applications to reside and also create a composer.json file inside this folder specifying the version of Solarium that needs to be installed.

```
{
  "require": {
    "solarium/solarium": "3.1.0"
  }
}
```

Now install Solarium by running the composer install command. Composer automatically downloads and installs Solarium and its related dependencies such as symfony event dispatcher. This can be seen in the output of Composer.

```
jayant@gamegeek: ~/htdocs/code                    _ □ X
                    jayant@gamegeek: ~/htdocs/code 70x21
jayant@gamegeek:~$ cd
jayant@gamegeek:~$ cd htdocs/code/
jayant@gamegeek:~/htdocs/code$ ls
composer.json
jayant@gamegeek:~/htdocs/code$ composer install
Loading composer repositories with package information
Installing dependencies (including require-dev)
  - Installing symfony/event-dispatcher (v2.2.3)
    Loading from cache

  - Installing solarium/solarium (3.1.0)
    Loading from cache

symfony/event-dispatcher suggests installing symfony/dependency-inject
ion (2.2.*)
symfony/event-dispatcher suggests installing symfony/http-kernel (2.2.
*)
Writing lock file
Generating autoload files
jayant@gamegeek:~/htdocs/code$ █
```

For installation on Windows, open up your command prompt and navigate to the Apache documentRoot folder. Create a new folder inside documentRoot and run composer install inside the folder.

We can see that during installation, `symfony event dispatcher` and `solarium library` are downloaded in a separate folder named `vendor`. Let us check the contents of the `vendor` folder. It consists of a file called `autoload.php` and three folders namely `composer`, `symfony`, and `solarium`. The `autoload.php` file contains the code to load Solarium library in our PHP code. Other folders are self explanatory. The `solarium` folders is the library and the `symfony` folder contains a dependency known as event dispatcher, which is being used by Solarium. The `composer` folder contains files which help in loading all the required libraries in PHP.

Executing ping queries on Solr using PHP and Solarium library

For using the Solarium library, we need to load the Solarium library in our PHP code. Let us see how to execute the same ping query that we fired earlier using PHP and Solarium.

 We have installed Solarium inside the `code` folder in our Apache `documentroot`. Apache `documentRoot` points to `~/htdocs` (inside our home folder).

First include the Solarium library in our code using the following line of code:

```
include_once("vendor/autoload.php");
```

Create a Solarium configuration array that defines how to connect to Solr.

```
$config = array(
  "endpoint" => array("localhost" => array("host"=>"127.0.0.1",
  "port"=>"8080", "path"=>"/solr", "core"=>"collection1",)
) );
```

Solarium has the concept of endpoints. An **endpoint** is basically a collection of settings that can be used to connect to a Solr server and a core. For each query that we execute via Solarium, we can specify an endpoint using which we want to execute the query. If no endpoint is specified, the query is executed using the first endpoint, which is the default endpoint. The benefit of using endpoints is that we need to create a single Solarium client instance irrespective of the number of servers or cores we use.

Create the Solarium client with the configuration we created earlier. And call the `createPing()` function to create the ping query.

```
$client = new Solarium\Client($config);

$ping = $client->createPing();
```

Finally execute the ping query and get the result using the following command:

```
$result = $client->ping($ping);

$result->getStatus();
```

It can be seen that the result is an array. But we can also call the `getStatus()` function to get the ping's status. We can execute the code using PHP command line or call the following URL to see the result:

```
http://localhost/code/pingSolarium.php
```

More about endpoints

Solarium provides us with the flexibility of adding multiple Solr servers as endpoints and using a single Solarium client to fire query on any Solr server. To add another endpoint to our Solarium configuration for Solr running on another port 8983 on our `localhost` and to use it to execute our query, we will use the following code:

```
$config = array(
  "endpoint" => array(
    "localhost" => array("host"=>"127.0.0.1",
     "port"=>"8080","path"=>"/solr", "core"=>"collection1",),
    "localhost2" => array("host"=>"127.0.0.1",
     "port"=>"8983","path"=>"/solr", "core"=>"collection1",)
  ) );
$result = $client->ping($ping, "localhost2");
```

The Solarium client provides functionality of adding and removing endpoints using the `addEndpoint(array $endpointConfig)` and `removeEndpoint(string $endpointName)` functions. To modify an endpoint during runtime, we can call `getEndpoint(String $endPointName)` to get the endpoint and the use functions such as `setHost(String $host)`, `setPort(int $port)`, `setPath(String $path)`, and `setCore(String $core)` to change the endpoint settings. Additional settings provided for endpoints are:

- The `setTimeout(int $timeout)` setting is used for specifying a timeout for a Solr connection

- The `setAuthentication(string $username, string $password)` setting is used for providing authentication if your Solr or Tomcat requires HTTP authentication
- The `setDefaultEndpoint(string $endpoint)` setting can be used to set the default endpoint for a Solarium client

Checking Solr query logs

We have now been able to execute a ping query on Solr using the Solarium library. To see how this works, open up Tomcat logs. It can be found at `<tomcat_path>/logs/solr.log` or `<tomcat_path>/logs/catalina.out`. On Linux, we can do a tail of the log to see fresh entries as they appear:

```
tail -f solr.log
```

On running the cURL-based PHP code that we wrote earlier, we can see the following hits in the log:

```
INFO  - 2013-06-25 19:51:16.389; org.apache.solr.core.SolrCore;
[collection1] webapp=/solr path=/admin/ping/ params={wt=json} hits=0
status=0 QTime=2
INFO  - 2013-06-25 19:51:16.390; org.apache.solr.core.SolrCore;
[collection1] webapp=/solr path=/admin/ping/ params={wt=json} status=0
QTime=3
```

On running the Solarium-based code, we get similar output but with an additional parameter `omitHeader=true`. This parameter causes the response header to be ignored in the output.

```
INFO  - 2013-06-25 19:53:03.534; org.apache.solr.core.SolrCore;
[collection1] webapp=/solr path=/admin/ping params={omitHeader=true&wt=js
on} hits=0 status=0 QTime=1
INFO  - 2013-06-25 19:53:03.534; org.apache.solr.core.SolrCore;
[collection1] webapp=/solr path=/admin/ping params={omitHeader=true&wt=js
on} status=0 QTime=1
```

So eventually, Solarium also creates a Solr URL and makes a cURL call to Solr to fetch the results. How does Solarium know which Solr server to hit? This information is provided in the endpoint settings in the `$config` parameter.

Solarium adapters

What about systems that do not have cURL installed? Solarium comes with a concept of **adapters**. Adapters define the way in which PHP will communicate with the Solr server. The default adapter is cURL, which we used earlier. But in the absence of cURL, the adapter can be switched to HTTP. **CurlAdapter** is dependent on the curl utility, which needs to be installed or enabled separately. **HttpAdapter** on the other hand uses the `file_get_contents()` PHP function to get a Solr response. This uses more memory and is not recommended when the numbers of queries on Solr are very large. Let us see the code to switch adapter in Solarium:

```
$client->setAdapter('Solarium\Core\Client\Adapter\Http');
var_dump($client->getAdapter());
```

We can call `getAdapter()` to check the current adapter. There are other adapters available—the **ZendHttp** adapter that is used with Zend Framework. There is a **PeclHttp** adapter, which uses the `pecl_http` package to make HTTP calls to Solr. The HTTP, Curl, and Pecl adapter support authentication, which can be used by the `setAuthentication()` function discussed earlier. **CurlAdapter** also supports the usage proxy. You can also create a custom adapter using the adapter interface if required.

Summary

We have successfully installed Solr as a part of Apache Tomcat server. We saw how to communicate with Solr using PHP and cURL but without using a library. We discussed a few libraries and concluded that Solarium is feature rich and an actively developed and maintained library. We were able to install Solarium and were able to communicate with Solr using PHP and Solarium library. We were able to see actual queries being executed on Solr in the Solr logs. We explored some features of the Solarium client library such as endpoints and adapters.

In the next chapter we will see how to use the Solarium library for inserting, updating, and deleting documents in Solr using our PHP code.

2
Inserting, Updating, and Deleting Documents from Solr

We will start this chapter by discussing the Solr schema. We will explore the default schema provided by Solr. Further, we will explore:

- Pushing sample data into Solr
- Adding sample documents to the Solr index
- Using PHP to add documents to the Solr index
- Updating documents in Solr using PHP
- Deleting documents in Solr using PHP
- Using commit, rollback, and index optimization

The Solr schema

The Solr schema mostly consists of fields and field types. It defines the fields that are to be stored in the Solr index and the processing that should happen on data being indexed or searched in those fields. Internally, the schema is used to assign properties to the fields used for creating a document that is to be indexed using the Lucene API. The default schema available with Solr can be located in `<solr_home>/example/solr/collection1/conf/schema.xml`. Here, `collection1` is the name of the core.

 A Solr server can have multiple cores and each core can have its own schema.

Let us open up the `schema.xml` file and go through it. In the XML file, we can see that there is a section for fields inside which there are multiple fields. Also, there is another section for types. The types section contains different entries of `fieldType`, which define the type of field in terms of how the field will be processed during indexing and during query. Let us understand how to create a `fieldType` entry.

The `fieldType` entry consists of a name attribute that is used in field definitions. The class attribute defines the behavior of the `fieldType` entry. Some other attributes are:

- `sortMissingLast`: If set to true this attribute will cause documents without the field to come after documents that have this field.

- `sortMissingFirst`: If set to true this attribute will cause documents without the field to come before documents that have this field.

- `precisionStep`: Lower values of `precisionstep` means more precisions, more terms in the index, larger index, and faster range queries. `0` disables indexing at different precision levels.

- `positionIncrementGap`: It defines the positions between the last token of one entry and the first token of next entry in a multivalued field. Let us take an example.

  Suppose there are two values in a multivalued field in a document. The first value is aa bb and the second value is xx yy. Ideally, the positions assigned to these tokens during indexing will be 0, 1, 2, and 3 for tokens aa, bb, xx, and yy respectively.

  A search for bb xx will give this document in its result. To prevent this from happening, we have to give a large `positionIncrementGap` say 100. Now the positions assigned to these tokens will be 0, 1, 100, and 101 for tokens aa, bb, xx, and yy. A search for bb xx will not give results as bb and xx are not near to each other.

The `FieldType` entries are either primitive such as `String`, `Int`, `Boolean`, `Double`, `Float`, or a derived field type. A derived field type can contain analyzer sections for defining the processing that will happen during either indexing or query. Each analyzer section consists of a single **tokenizer** and multiple filters. They define how data is processed. For example, there is a `fieldType` text_ws where the **analyzer** is a `WhiteSpaceTokenizerFactory`. So any data being indexed or searched in a field of the text_ws type will have the data broken over white space into multiple tokens. Another `fieldType` text_general has separate analyzer entries for indexes and queries. During analysis for indexing the data is passed through a tokenizer known as `StandardTokenizerFactory` and then through multiple filters. Following are filters that we use:

- `StopFilterFactory`: This filters are used for removal of stop words that are defined in `stopwords.txt`
- `SynonymFilterFactory`: This filters are used for assigning synonyms to words that are defined in `index_synonyms.txt`
- `LowerCaseFilterFactory`: This filter is used for converting the text in all the tokens to lowercase

Similarly, there are different analyses happening to the query on this field during search. And that is defined by the analyzer of the type query.

Most of the field types that are required are generally provided in the default schema. But we can go ahead and create a new field type if we feel a need for it.

Each field consists of a name and a type, which are mandatory, and some other attributes. Let's run through the attributes:

- `name`: This attribute displays the name of the field.
- `type`: This attribute defines the type of the field. All types are defined as the `fieldType` entries we discussed before.
- `indexed`: This attribute is true if the data in this field has to be indexed. The text in indexed fields is broken into tokens and an index is created from the tokens, which can be used for searching the document based on these tokens.
- `stored`: This attribute is true if the data in this field also needs to be stored. Data that has been indexed cannot be used to construct the original text. So text in fields are stored separately for retrieving original text of the document.
- `multivalued`: This attribute is true if the field contains multiple values within a single document. An example of multiple values associated with a document is **tags**. A document can have multiple tags and for search on any of the tags, the same document has to be returned.
- `required`: This attribute is true if the field is mandatory to be populated for every document during index creation.

In addition to normal fields, the schema consists of some dynamic fields, which add flexibility in defining the field's names. For example, a dynamic field by the name of `*_i` will match any field ending with _i, for example, `genre_i` or `xyz_i`.

Some other sections in the schema are:

- **uniqueKey**: This section defines a field to be unique and mandatory. This field will be used to enforce uniqueness among all documents.

- **copyField**: This section can be used to copy multiple fields into a single field. So we can have multiple text fields with different field types and a super field where all text fields are copied for a generic search among all fields.

Adding sample documents to the Solr index

Let us push in some sample data into Solr. Go to `<solr_dir>/example/ exampledocs`. Execute the following commands to add all sample documents into our Solr index:

```
java -Durl=http://localhost:8080/solr/update -Dtype=application/csv -jar
post.jar books.csv
```

```
java -Durl=http://localhost:8080/solr/update  -jar post.jar *.xml
```

```
java -Durl=http://localhost:8080/solr/update -Dtype=application/json -jar
post.jar books.json
```

To check how many documents have been indexed go to the following URL:

```
http://localhost:8080/solr/collection1/select/?q=*:*
```

This is a query to Solr that asks to return all the documents in the index. The `numFound` field in the XML output specifies the number of documents in our Solr index.

```
localhost:8080/solr/colle    ×
           localhost:8 ⤻  ⊙  ☆       ✿  ⊕  ⊖  ⚙  🖼  ⊙  ▽       ≡

This XML file does not appear to have any style information associated with it. The
document tree is shown below.

▼<response>
  ▼<lst name="responseHeader">
     <int name="status">0</int>
     <int name="QTime">1294</int>
    ▼<lst name="params">
       <str name="q">*:*</str>
     </lst>
   </lst>
  ▼<result name="response" numFound="63" start="0">
    ▼<doc>
       <str name="id">978-0641723445</str>
      ▼<arr name="cat">
         <str>book</str>
         <str>hardcover</str>
       </arr>
       <str name="name">The Lightning Thief</str>
       <str name="author">Rick Riordan</str>
       <str name="author_s">Rick Riordan</str>
       <str name="series_t">Percy Jackson and the Olympians</str>
       <int name="sequence_i">1</int>
       <str name="genre_s">fantasy</str>
       <bool name="inStock">true</bool>
       <float name="price">12.5</float>
       <str name="price_c">12.50,USD</str>
       <int name="pages_i">384</int>
       <long name="_version_">1438729999866658816</long>
     </doc>
    ▼<doc>
```

We are working with the default schema. To check the schema, go to the
following URL:

```
http://localhost:8080/solr/#/collection1/schema
```

The following screenshot shows the content of a sample schema file `schema.xml`:

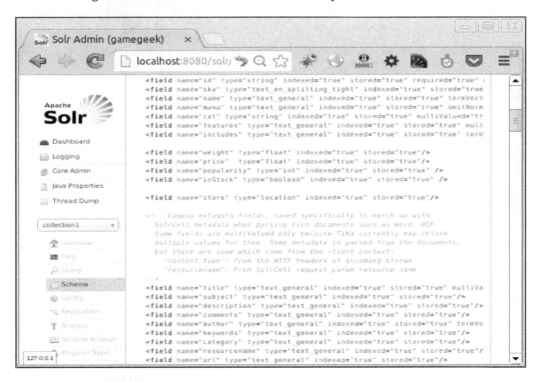

We can see that there are multiple fields: id, title, subject, description, author, and others. Configuring Solr is all about designing the schema to suit the field requirements. We can also see that the id field is unique.

We can insert documents in Solr via the post.jar program as seen earlier. To do this, we would need to create an XML, CSV, or JSON file specifying the fields and values in the document. Once the file is ready, we can simply call one of the earlier mentioned commands to insert the document in the file into Solr. The XML format for the file is as follows:

```
<add>
  <doc>
      <field name="id">0553573403</field>
      <field name="cat">book</field>
      <field name="name">A game of thrones</field>
      <!--add more fields -->
  </doc>
  <!-- add more docs here -->
</add>
```

The `post.jar` file is a program for processing multiple documents in a file. We can use it if we have a large number of documents to insert and the documents are in a CSV, XML, or JSON format. The PHP code used to insert documents in Solr in turn creates a Solr URL and makes a `curl` call with appropriate data.

```
curl http://localhost:8080/solr/update?commit=true -H "Content-Type:
text/xml" --data-binary '<add><doc><field name="id">...</field></
doc>...</add>'
```

Using PHP to add documents to the Solr index

Let us see the code to add documents to Solr using the Solarium library. When we execute the following query we can see that there are three books of the author *George R R Martin* in our Solr index:

```
http://localhost:8080/solr/collection1/select/?q=martin
```

Let us add the remaining two books, which have also been published to our index:

1. Create a solarium client using the following code:

   ```
   $client = new Solarium\Client($config);
   ```

2. Create an instance of the update query using the following code:

   ```
   $updateQuery = $client->createUpdate();
   ```

3. Create the documents you want to add and add fields to the document.

   ```
   $doc1 = $updateQuery->createDocument();
   $doc1->id = 112233445;
   $doc1->cat = 'book';
   $doc1->name = 'A Feast For Crows';
   $doc1->price = 8.99;
   $doc1->inStock = 'true';
   $doc1->author = 'George R.R. Martin';
   $doc1->series_t = '"A Song of Ice and Fire"';
   $doc1->sequence_i = 4;
   $doc1->genre_s = 'fantasy';
   ```

4. Similarly, another document `$doc2` can be created.

 Note that the `id` field is unique. So we will have to keep different `id` field for different documents that we add to Solr.

5. Add documents to the update query followed by the `commit` command:
```
$updateQuery->addDocuments(array($doc1, $doc2));
$updateQuery->addCommit();
```

6. Finally, execute the following query:
```
$result = $client->update($updateQuery);
```

7. Let us execute the code using the following command:
```
php insertSolr.php
```

   After executing the code, the search for martin gives five results

8. To add a single document, we can call the `addDocument` function to the update query instance using the following line of code:
```
$updateQuery->addDocument($doc1);
```

Updating documents in Solr using PHP

Let us see how we can use PHP code along with Solarium library to update documents in Solr.

1. First check if there are any documents with the word `smith` in our index.
```
http://localhost:8080/solr/collection1/select/?q=smith
```

2. We can see `numFound=0`, which means that there are no such documents. Let us add a book to our index with the last name of the author as `smith`.
```
$updateQuery = $client->createUpdate();
$testdoc = $updateQuery->createDocument();
$testdoc->id = 123456789;
$testdoc->cat = 'book';
$testdoc->name = 'Test book';
$testdoc->price = 5.99;
$testdoc->author = 'Hello Smith';
$updateQuery->addDocument($testdoc);
$updateQuery->addCommit();
$client->update($updateQuery);
```

3. If we run the same select query again, we can see that now there is one document in our index with the author as Smith. Let us now update the author's name to Jack Smith and the price tag to 7.59:

```
$testdoc = $updateQuery->createDocument();
$testdoc->id = 123456789;
$testdoc->cat = 'book';
$testdoc->name = 'Test book';
$testdoc->price = 7.59;
$testdoc->author = 'Jack Smith';
$updateQuery->addDocument($testdoc, true);
$updateQuery->addCommit();
$client->update($updateQuery);
```

4. On running the same query again, we can see that now the author name and price is updated in our index on Solr.

The process to update a document in Solr is similar to that of adding a document in Solr except for the fact that we have to set the overwrite flag to true. If no parameter is set, Solarium will not pass any flag to Solr. But on the Solr end, the overwrite flag is by default set to true. So any document to Solr will replace a previous document with the same unique key.

Solr internally does not have an update command. In order to update a document, when we provide the unique key and the overwrite flag, Solr internally deletes and inserts the document again.

We will need to add all fields of the document again, even fields that are not required to be updated. Since Solr will be deleting the complete document and inserting the new document.

Another interesting parameter in the method signature is the commit within time.

```
$updateQuery->addDocument($doc1, $overwrite=true, $commitwithin=10000)
```

The preceding code asks Solr to overwrite the document and commit within 10 seconds. This is explained later in this chapter.

We can also use the addDocuments(array($doc1, $doc2)) command to update multiple documents in a single call.

Deleting documents in Solr using PHP

Now let us go ahead and delete this document from Solr.

```
$deleteQuery = $client->createUpdate();
$deleteQuery->addDeleteQuery('author:Smith');
$deleteQuery->addCommit();
$client->update($deleteQuery);
```

Now, if we run the following query on Solr, the document is not found:

```
http://localhost:8080/solr/collection1/select/?q=smith
```

What we did here was that we created a query in Solr to search for all documents where the author field contains the smith word and then passed it as a delete query.

We can add multiple delete queries via the addDeleteQueries method. This can be used to delete multiple sets of documents in a single call.

```
$deleteQuery->addDeleteQuery(array('author:Burst',
'author:Alexander'));
```

When this query is executed, all documents where the author field is either Burst or Alexander are deleted from the index.

In addition to deleting by a query, we can also delete by ID. Each book that we have added to our index has an id field, which we have marked as unique. To delete by ID, simply call the addDeleteById($id) function.

```
$deleteQuery->addDeleteById('123456789');
```

We can also use the addDeleteByIds(array $ids) to delete multiple documents in a single go.

> In addition to using PHP code to delete documents, we can also use curl calls to delete a document by ID or by query. The curl call to delete by ID is as follows:
>
> ```
> curl http://localhost:8080/solr/collection1/
> update?commitWithin=1000 -H "Content-Type: text/xml"
> --data-binary '<delete><id>123456789</id></delete>'
> ```
>
> And the curl call to delete by query is as follows:
>
> ```
> curl http://localhost:8080/solr/collection1/
> update?commitWithin=1000 -H "Content-Type: text/xml"
> --data-binary '<delete><query>author:smith</query></
> delete>'
> ```

Here is a simple way of deleting all documents from the Solr index:

```
curl http://localhost:8080/solr/collection1/update?commitWithin=1000 -H
"Content-Type: text/xml" --data-binary '<delete><query>*:*</query></
delete>'
```

Commit, rollback, and index optimization

The commitWithin parameter that we have been passing as arguments to our addDocument() function specifies the time for the commit to happen for this add document operation. This leaves the control of when to do the commit to Solr itself. Solr optimizes the number of commits to a minimum while still fulfilling the update latency requirements.

The rollback option is exposed via the addRollback() function. Rollback can be done since the last commit and before current commit. Once a commit has been done, the changes cannot be rolled back.

```
$rollbackQuery = $client->createUpdate();
$rollbackQuery->addRollback();
```

Index optimization is one of the tasks that is not necessarily required. But an optimized index has better performance than a non-optimized index. To optimize an index using the PHP code, we can use the addOptimize(boolean $softCommit, boolean $waitSearcher, int $maxSegments) function. It has parameters to enable soft commit, wait until a new searcher is opened and number of segments to optimize to. Also note that index optimization slows down the execution of all other queries on Solr.

```
$updateQuery = $client->createUpdate();
$updateQuery->addOptimize($softcommit=true, $waitSearcher=false,
$maxSegments=10)
```

For more advanced options, we can also use the addParam() function to add key value pairs to the query string.

```
$updateQuery->addParam('name', 'value');
```

It is generally advisable to combine multiple commands in a single request. The commands are executed in the order in which they are added to the request. But we should also take care not to build huge queries that exceed the limit of a request. Use rollbacks in exception scenarios to avoid partial updates/deletes when running bulk queries and perform commit separately.

```
try
{
    $client->update($updateQuery);
}catch(Solarium\Exception $e)
{
    $rollbackQuery = $client->createUpdate();
    $rollbackQuery->addRollback();
    $client->update($rollbackQuery);
}
$commitQry = $client->createUpdate();
$commitQry->addCommit();
$client->update($commitQry);
```

In the preceding piece of code if the `update` query throws an exception, then it is rolled back.

Summary

In this chapter we started off by discussing the Solr schema. We got a basic understanding of how the Solr schema works. We then added some sample documents to our Solr index. Then we saw multiple pieces of code to add, update, and delete documents to our Solr index. We also saw how to use cURL to delete documents. We discussed how commit and rollback work on the Solr index. We also saw an example of how to use rollback in our code. We discussed index optimization using PHP code and the benefits of optimizing the Solr index.

In the next chapter we will see how to execute search queries on Solr using PHP code and explore different query modes available with Solr.

3
Select Query on Solr and Query Modes (DisMax/eDisMax)

This chapter will cover how to execute a basic select query on the Solr index using PHP and the Solarium library. We will be specifying different query parameters such as number of rows to fetch, fetching specific fields, sorting, and some other parameters in the Solarium query. We will discuss what query modes (query parsers) in Solr are and will also go through the different query modes available in Solr and their usage. We will look at different features to improve the results from our query or get more specific results from our query. The topics that will be covered are as follows:

- Creating a basic select query with sorting and return fields
- Running queries using select configuration
- Re-using queries
- DisMax and eDisMax query modes
- Component-based architecture of Solarium
- Executing queries using DisMax and eDisMax
- Date boosting in eDisMax
- Advanced tuning parameters

Creating a basic select query with sorting and return fields

Using the following query, let us look for all the books in our index and return the top five results in JSON format:

```
http://localhost:8080/solr/collection1/select/?q=cat:book&rows=5&wt=j
son
```

As seen earlier, we can form a query URL and use cURL to fire the query via PHP. Decode the JSON response and use it as result.

Let us look at the Solarium code to execute `select` queries on Solr. Create a `select` query from the Solarium client as follows:

```
$query = $client->createSelect();
```

Create a query to search for all books:

```
$query->setQuery('cat:book');
```

Suppose we show three results per page. So on the second page, we will start from four and display the next three results.

```
$query->setStart(3)->setRows(3);
```

Set which fields should be returned using the following code:

```
$query->setFields(array('id','name','price','author'));
```

> PHP 5.4 users can use square brackets to construct an array instead of the earlier `array(...)` construct.
> ```
> $query->setFields(['id','name','price','author']);
> ```

Let us sort the result by price using the following query:

```
$query->addSort('price',$query::SORT_ASC);
```

Finally, execute the following `select` query and get the result:

```
$resultSet = $client->select($query);
```

The resultset contains an array of documents. And each document is an object containing fields and values. For a multivalued field in Solr, all values will be returned as an array. We will need to handle the values accordingly. In addition to the four fields that we retrieved using our query, we also get the score of the document. The document score is a number calculated by Lucene to rank the documents based on their relevance with respect to the input query. We will talk in depth about scoring in later chapters. Let us iterate over the resultset and display the fields.

```
foreach($resultSet as $doc)
{
  echo PHP_EOL."-------".PHP_EOL;
  echo PHP_EOL."ID : ".$doc->id;
  echo PHP_EOL."Name : ".$doc->name;
  echo PHP_EOL."Author : ".$doc->author;
  echo PHP_EOL."Price : ".$doc->price;
  echo PHP_EOL."Score : ".$doc->score;
}
```

From the resultset, we can also get the number of documents found using the `getNumFound()` function as follows:

```
$found = $resultSet->getNumFound();
```

Internally, the parameters that we set are used to form a Solr query and the same query is executed on Solr. We can check the query being executed from the Solr logs.

 Solr logs are located in the `<tomcat_home>/logs` folder in the `catalina.out` file.

The executed query looks as follows:

```
7643159 [http-bio-8080-exec-2] INFO  org.apache.solr.core.SolrCore  -
[collection1] webapp=/solr path=/select params={omitHeader=true&sort
=price+asc&fl=id,name,price,author&start=2&q=cat:book&wt=json&rows=5}
hits=15 status=0 QTime=1
```

The parameter for the `setQuery()` function should be equal to the q parameter in our Solr query. If we want to search on multiple fields in our Solr index, we will have to create the search query with the required fields. For example, if we want to search for Author as Martin and Category as book, our `setQuery()` function will be as follows:

```
$query->setQuery('cat:book AND author:Martin');
```

Running a query using select configuration

In addition to building the `select` query through functions, it is also possible to build a `select` query using an array of key-value pairs. Here is a `selectconfig` query with parameters for the preceding query:

```
$selectConfig = array(
   'query' => 'cat:book AND author:Martin',
   'start' => 3,
   'rows' => 3,
   'fields' => array('id','name','price','author'),
   'sort' => array('price' => 'asc')
);
```

We can also add multiple sorting fields as an array using the `addSorts(array $sorts)` function. To sort by price and then by score, we can use the following parameters in the `addSorts()` function:

```
$query->addSorts(array('price'=>'asc','score'=>'desc'));
```

We can use the `getQuery()` function to get the query parameter. And the `getSorts()` function to get the sorting parameter from our select query. We can also use the `removeField($fieldStr)` and `removeSort($sortStr)` functions to remove parameters from the fields list and sort list of our query.

We can use the `setQueryDefaultField(String $field)` and `setQueryDefaultOperator(String $operator)` functions to change the default query field and default operator in our Solr query. If the functions are not provided, the default query field and default query operator are picked up from the Solr configuration. The default search field is picked up from the `df` parameter in `solrconfig.xml`. The default operator is `OR` if not provided. It can be overwritten by passing the `q.op` parameter in the query.

Re-using queries

In most cases, the queries that you build as a part of the application can be reused. It would make more sense to re-use the queries instead of creating them again. The functions provided by the Solarium interface help in modifying the Solarium query for re-use. Let us see an example for re-using queries.

Suppose we form a complex query based on input parameters. For pagination purposes, we would like to use the same query but change the start and rows parameters to fetch the next or previous page. Another case where a query could be reused is sorting. Suppose we would like to sort by price in ascending order and later by descending order.

Let us first define and create an alias for Solarium namespaces we will be using in our code.

```
use Solarium\Client;
use Solarium\QueryType\Select\Query\Query as Select;
```

Next, create a class that extends the Solarium query interface:

```
Class myQuery extends Select
{
```

Inside the class we will create the init() function, which will override the same function in the parent class and add our default query parameters there as follows:

```
protected function init()
{
  parent::init();
  $this->setQuery('*:*');
  $this->setFields(array('id','name','price','author','score'));
  $this->setStart($this->getPageStart(1));
  $this->setRows($this->RESULTSPERPAGE);
  $this->addSort('price', $this->getSortOrder('asc'));
}
```

RESULTSPERPAGE is a private variable that can be declared as 5. Create a separate function to set the query.

```
function setMyQuery($query)
{
  $this->setQuery($query);
}
```

Create a function to reset the sorting. A reset would mean removing all previous sorting parameters.

```
private function resetSort()
{
  $sorts = $this->getSorts();
  foreach($sorts as $sort)
  {
    $this->removeSort($sort);
  }
}
```

Changing sorting parameters includes resetting the current sort and adding a new sorting parameter.

```
function changeSort($sortField, $sortOrder)
{
    $this->resetSort();
    $this->addSort($sortField, $this->getSortOrder($sortOrder));
}
```

A function to add additional sorting parameters is used as follows:

```
function addMoreSort($sortField, $sortOrder)
{
    $this->addSort($sortField, $this->getSortOrder($sortOrder));
}
```

A function to change the page is used as follows:

```
function goToPage($pgno)
{
    $this->setStart($this->getPageStart($pgno));
}
```

Once the class is defined, we can create an instance of the class and set our initial query. This will give us results from the first page.

```
$query = new myQuery();
$query->setMyQuery('cat:book');
echo "<b><br/>Searching for all books</b>".PHP_EOL;
$resultSet = $client->select($query);
displayResults($resultSet);
```

To go to any other page, simply call the goToPage() function that we have created with the page we want to go to. It will alter the Solarium query, and change the Start parameter to coincide with results for the page.

```
$query->goToPage(3);
echo "<b><br/>Going to page 3</b>".PHP_EOL;
$resultSet = $client->select($query);
displayResults($resultSet);
```

The complete code is available as part of downloads. What we have done here is extend the query interface and add our own functions to change the query, reset and add sorting parameters, and for pagination. Once we have an object of the myQuery class, all we have to do is keep on altering the parameters as required and keep on executing the query with the altered parameters.

DisMax and eDisMax query modes

DisMax (Disjunction Max)and **eDisMax (Extended Disjunction Max)** are query modes in Solr. They define the way how Solr parses user input to query different fields and with different relevance weights. eDisMax is an improvement over the DisMax query mode. DisMax and eDisMax are by default enabled in our Solr configuration. To switch the query type we need to specify `defType=dismax` or `defType=edismax` in our Solr query.

Let us add some more books to our index. Execute the following command in our `<solr dir>/example/exampledocs` folder (`books.csv` is available in code downloads):

```
java -Durl=http://localhost:8080/solr/update -Dtype=application/csv -jar
post.jar books.csv
```

DisMax handles most queries. But there are still some cases where DisMax is unable to provide results. It is advisable to use eDisMax in those cases. The DisMax query parser does not support the default Lucene query syntax. But that syntax is supported in eDisMax. Let us check it out.

To search for `books` in `cat`, let us execute the following query:

```
http://localhost:8080/solr/collection1/select?start=0&q=cat:book&rows=
15&defType=dismax
```

We will be getting zero results because the query `q=cat:book` is not supported by DisMax. To execute this query in DisMax, we will have to specify an additional query parameter `qf` (query fields) as follows:

```
http://localhost:8080/solr/collection1/select?start=0&q=book&qf=cat&ro
ws=15&defType=dismax
```

But `q=cat:book` will work on eDisMax:

```
http://localhost:8080/solr/collection1/select?start=0&q=cat:book&rows=
15&defType=edismax
```

To understand how the Solarium library can be used for executing DisMax and eDisMax queries, we need to introduce the concept of **components**. Solr query has lots of options. Putting all options in a single query model can cause decreased performance. So, additional functionality is broken down into components. The query model of Solarium handles basic queries, and additional functionality can be added to the query by using components. Components are only loaded when used thus improving performance. The component structure allows for easy addition of more components.

Executing queries using DisMax and eDisMax

Let us explore how to execute DisMax and eDisMax queries using the Solarium library. First, get a DisMax component from our select query using the following code:

```
$dismax = $query->getDisMax();
```

Boosting is used in Solr to alter the score of some documents in a resultset, so that certain documents are ranked higher than others based on their content. A boost query is a raw query string that is inserted along with the user's query to boost certain documents in the result. We can set a boost on author = martin. This query will boost results where author contains martin by 2.

```
$dismax->setBoostQuery('author:martin^2');
```

Query fields specify the fields to query with certain boosts. The query string passed in setQuery function is matched against text in these fields. When a field is boosted, a match for a query text in that field is given more importance and so that document is ranked higher. In the following function, matches in the author field are boosted by 3, where as matches in name are boosted by 2 and the cat field has no boost. So during search, the document in which the input query text matches with that in author is ranked higher compared to documents where text is found in the name or cat fields.

```
$dismax->setQueryFields('cat name^2 author^3');
```

By default, all clauses in the default Solr query are treated as optional, unless they are specified by a + or - sign. Optional clauses are interpreted as any one of the clauses in the query should match with the text in the specified fields in the document to consider that document to be a part of the search result. When dealing with optional clauses, the minimum match parameter says that some minimum number of clauses must match. The minimum number of clauses can be a number or a percentage. In case of a number irrespective of the number of clauses in the query the minimum specified must match. In case of a percentage, a number is computed from the available number of clauses and the percentage and it is rounded down to the nearest integer and then used.

```
$dismax->setMinimumMatch('70%');
```

Phrase query fields are used to boost the score of documents in case the terms in the query parameter appear in close proximity. The closer the query terms are in the Phrase query field, the higher is the score of the document. In the following code, this score is being boosted by 5 giving higher relevance to these documents:

```
$dismax->setPhraseFields('series_t^5');
```

Phrase slop is the number of positions a token has to be moved in relation to another token in order to match a phrase specified in the query. During indexing the input text is analyzed and broken into smaller words or phrases that are known as **tokens**. Similarly during search, the input query is broken into tokens that are matched with tokens in the index. This is used in conjunction to the Phrase fields to specify the slop to apply to queries with the Phrase fields set.

```
$dismax->setPhraseSlop('2');
```

Query slop specifies the slop permitted in phrases in the user's input query.

```
$dismax->setQueryPhraseSlop('1');
```

eDisMax has all features of the DisMax parser and extends it.

All of the preceding mentioned functions will also work with eDisMax queries. All we have to do is get the eDisMax component and call these functions on the eDisMax component. To get the eDisMax component, call the getEDisMax() function as follows:

```
$edismax = $query->getEDisMax();
```

In addition to this, field-based queries similar to that supported by the basic Solr query parser are also supported in eDisMax and they give us better flexibility in creating our search query.

eDisMax provides us with the option of applying a boost function with multiplicative effect. We can use the setBoostFunctionsMult() function to provide a boost function that will multiply with the score. The DisMax parser on the other hand provides the setBoostFunctions() function, which can influence the score by adding the resultant boost of the function to the score of the query.

eDisMax provides some other functions such as setPhraseBigramFields(), which chops the user query into bigrams and queries the fields specified with the related boost. For example, if the user has entered hello world solr, it will be broken into hello world and world solr and executed on the fields specified in these functions. Similarly, another setPhraseTrigramFields() function can be used to break the user input into trigrams instead of bigrams. Trigrams would contain three-word phrases instead of the two-word phrases we saw earlier in bigrams. eDisMax also provides functions such as setPhraseBigramSlop() and setPhraseTrigramSlop() to specify custom slop with respect to the bigram and trigram fields during search.

Slop is the number of positions a token has to be moved with respect to another to get a match. A slop of 5 between tokens t1 and t2 would mean that t1 should occur within five tokens of t2.

Let us look at the Solr query logs for DisMax and eDisMax queries.

```
43782622 [http-bio-8080-exec-5] INFO  org.apache.solr.core.SolrCore  -
[collection1] webapp=/solr path=/select params={mm=70%25&tie=0.1&qf=ca
t+name^2+author^3&q.alt=*:*&wt=json&rows=25&defType=edismax&omitHeader
=true&pf=series_t^5&bq=author:martin^2&fl=id,name,price,author,score&s
tart=0&q=book+-harry+"dark+tower"&qs=1&ps=2} hits=24 status=0 QTime=55

43795018 [http-bio-8080-exec-1] INFO  org.apache.solr.core.SolrCore  -
[collection1] webapp=/solr path=/select params={mm=70%25&tie=0.1&qf=ca
t+name^2+author^3&q.alt=*:*&wt=json&rows=25&defType=dismax&omitHeader=
true&pf=series_t^5&bq=author:martin^2&fl=id,name,price,author,score&st
art=0&q=book+-harry+"dark+tower"&qs=1&ps=2} hits=24 status=0 QTime=2
```

We can see that in addition to the normal parameters of Solr query, there is a `defType` parameter that specifies the type of query. In the preceding case, we can see that `defType` is DisMax or eDisMax depending on the type of query we executed.

Date boosting in an eDisMax query

Let us use eDisMax to boost the results of a search based on date so that the most recent book appears on top. We will use the `setBoostFunctionsMult()` function to specify the boost on `modified_date`, which in our case stores the date when the record was last added or updated.

```
$query = $client->createSelect();
$query->setQuery('cat:book -author:martin');
$edismax = $query->getedismax();
$edismax->setBoostFunctionsMult('recip(ms(NOW,last_modified),1,1,1)');
$resultSet = $client->select($query);
```

Here we are searching for all books where the author is not named Martin (`martin`). The – (negative sign) is meant for *not query*. And we have added a multiplicative boost on the reciprocal of the date between today and last modified date. The `recip` function provided by Solr is defined as follows:

```
recip(x,m,a,b) = a/(m*x+b) which in our case becomes 1/(1*ms(NOW,last_
modified)+1)
```

Here `m`, `a`, and `b` are constants, `x` can be any numeric value or complex function. In our case, `x` is the number of milliseconds between `NOW` and `last_modified`. We are adding 1 in the denominator to avoid errors in cases where `last_modified` is not present. This shows that as the difference between `NOW` and `last_modified` increases the boost for that document decreases. Recent documents have higher `last_modified` and so the difference with respect to `NOW` is less and so boost is more. Let us check the Solr logs for the query.

```
2889948 [http-bio-8080-exec-4] INFO  org.apache.solr.core.SolrCore  -
[collection1] webapp=/solr path=/select params={mm=70%25&tie=0.1&pf2
=name^2+author^1.8+series_t^1.3&q.alt=*:*&wt=json&rows=25&defType=ed
ismax&omitHeader=true&pf=series_t^5&fl=id,name,price,author,score,la
st_modified&start=0&q=cat:book+-author:martin&boost=recip(ms(NOW,last_
modified),1,1,1)} hits=26 status=0 QTime=59
```

Copy and paste the parameters from the query in Solr log and append to the Solr
`select` URL. Also change `wt=json` to `wt=csv`. This will give a comma separated
view of the results.

```
http://localhost:8080/solr/collection1/select?mm=70%25&tie=0.1&pf2=
name^2+author^1.8+series_t^1.3&q.alt=*:*&wt=csv&rows=25&defType=edi
smax&omitHeader=true&pf=series_t^5&fl=id,name,price,author,score,la
st_modified&start=0&q=cat:book+-author:martin&boost=recip(ms(NOW,last_
modified),1,1,1)
```

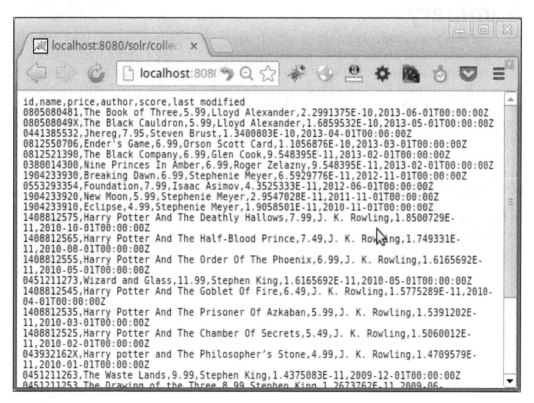

The URL can be altered further to tune/modify the query as per our requirement.

Advanced query parameters

Alternative queries are used when the query parameter is either blank or not specified. Solarium by default sets the query parameter as *:*. Alternative queries can be used to get all documents from an index for faceting purposes.

```
$dismax->setQueryAlternative('*:*');
```

For selecting all documents in DisMax/eDisMax, the normal query syntax *:* does not work. To select all documents, set the default query value in Solarium query to empty string. This is required as the default query in Solarium is *:*. Also set the alternative query to *:*. DisMax/eDisMax normal query syntax does not support *:*, but the alternative query syntax does.

Summary

We were able to execute select queries on Solr using the Solarium library. We explored the basic parameters for the select query. We saw how to use a configuration array to create a Solarium query. We were able to iterate through the results after executing a query. We extended the query class to re-use queries. We were able to do pagination on our existing query and were able to change the sorting parameters without recreating the complete query again. We saw DisMax and eDisMax query modes in Solr. We also got an idea of the component based structure of Solarium library. We explored the query parameters for DisMax and eDisMax queries. We also saw how to use an eDisMax query to do "recent first" date boosting on Solr. Finally, we saw some advanced query parameters for DisMax and eDisMax in Solarium.

In the next chapter, we will go deeper into advanced queries based on different criteria from our query result.

Advanced Queries – Filter Queries and Faceting

This chapter starts by defining filter queries and their benefits compared to the normal search queries that we have used earlier. We will see how we can use filter queries in Solr with PHP and the Solarium library. We will then explore faceting in Solr. We will also see how PHP can be used to facet in Solr. We will explore faceting by field, faceting by query, and faceting by range. We will also look at faceting by using pivots. The topics that will be covered are as follows:

- Filter queries and their benefits
- Executing filter queries using PHP and Solarium
- Creating a filter query configuration
- Faceting
- Faceting by field, query, and range
- Faceting pivots

Filter queries and their benefits

Filter queries are used to put a **filter** on the results from a Solr query without affecting the score. Suppose we are looking for all books that are in stock. The related query will be `q=cat:book AND inStock:true`.

```
http://localhost:8080/solr/collection1/select/?q=cat:book%20AND%20inSt
ock:true&fl=id,name,price,author,score,inStock&rows=50&defType=edismax
```

Another way to handle the same query is by using filter queries. The query will change to `q=cat:book&fq=inStock:true`.

```
http://localhost:8080/solr/collection1/select/?q=cat:book&fl=id,name,p
rice,author,score,inStock&rows=50&fq=inStock:true&defType=edismax
```

Though the results are the same, there are certain benefits of using filter queries. A filter query stores only document IDs. This makes it very fast to apply filters to include or exclude documents in a query. A normal query on the other hand has a complex scoring function causing reduced performance. Scoring or relevance calculation and ranking is not done on a filter query. Another benefit of using filter queries is that they are cached at Solr level resulting in an even better performance. It is recommended to use filter queries instead of normal queries.

Executing filter queries

To add a filter query to our existing query, first we need to create a filter query from our Solr query module.

```
$query = $client->createSelect();
$query->setQuery('cat:book');
$fquery = $query->createFilterQuery('Availability');
```

The string provided as a parameter to the `createFilterQuery()` function is used as *key* for the filter query. This key can be used to retrieve the filter query associated with this query. Once the filter query module is available, we can use the `setQuery()` function to set a filter query for this Solarium query.

In the preceding piece of code, we have created a filter query by the name of `Availability`. We will set the filter query for key `Availability` as `instock:true` and then execute the complete query as follows:

```
$fquery->setQuery('inStock:true');
$resultSet = $client->select($query);
```

Once the resultset is available, it can be iterated over to get and process the results.

Let us check Solr logs and see the query that was sent to Solr.

```
70981712 [http-bio-8080-exec-8] INFO  org.apache.solr.core.SolrCore  -
[collection1] webapp=/solr path=/select params={mm=70%25&tie=0.1&pf2=
name^2+author^1.8+series_t^1.3&q.alt=*:*&wt=json&rows=25&defType=edis
max&omitHeader=true&pf=series_t^5&fl=id,name,price,author,score,last_
modified&start=0&q=cat:book+-author:martin&boost=recip(ms(NOW,last_mod
ified),1,1,1)&fq=inStock:true} hits=19 status=0 QTime=4
```

We can see the `fq` parameter `inStock:true` appended to the parameter list of our Solr query.

The `getFilterQuery(string $key)` function can be used to retrieve the filter query associated with a Solarium query.

```
echo $fquery->getFilterQuery('Availability')->getQuery();
```

Creating filter query configuration

We can also pass filter query as a configuration parameter to the Solarium query using the `addFilterQuery()` function. For this, we need to first define the filter query as a configuration array and then add it to the Solarium query.

```
$fqconfig = array(
        "query"=>"inStock:true",
        "key"=>"Availability",
    );
$query = $client->createSelect();
$query->addFilterQuery($fqconfig);
```

The Solr query created by the preceding configuration is similar to the one created earlier. The benefit of using filter query configuration is that we can define multiple standard filter queries as configurations and add them in our Solr query as required. The `addTag(String $tag)` and `addTags(array $tags)` functions are used to define tags in the filter queries. We can use these tags to exclude certain filter queries in facets. We will go through an example later.

Faceting

Faceted searches break up the search results into multiple categories, showing counts for each category. Faceting is used in searches to drill down into a subset of results from a query. To get an idea of how facets are helpful, let us go to www.amazon.com and search for mobile phones. We will see facets on the left-hand side such as brand, display size, and carrier. Once we select a facet to drill down, we will see more facets that will help us narrow down the phone we would like to purchase.

Faceting is generally done on human readable text that is predefined such as location, price, and author name. It would not make sense tokenizing these fields. So, *facet fields* are kept separate from search and sorting fields in the Solr schema. They are also not converted to lowercase but are kept as they are. Faceting is done on indexed fields on Solr. So there is no need to store faceted fields.

Solarium introduces the concept of **facetset**, which is one central component and can be used to create and manage facets and also set global facet options. Let us push the `books.csv` file from this chapter into the Solr index. We can use the same command that was used in *Chapter 2, Inserting, Updating, and Deleting Documents from Solr*, which is as follows:

```
java -Durl=http://localhost:8080/solr/update -Dtype=application/csv -jar
post.jar books.csv
```

Facet by field

Faceting by field counts the number of occurrences of a term in a specific field. Let us create facets on **author** and **genre**. There are separate string fields in our Solr index for indexing facet-related strings without any tokenization. In this case, the fields are `author_s` and `genre_s`.

 Fields ending with _s are dynamic fields defined in our Solr `schema.xml`. Dynamic fields defined as `*_s` match any field that ends in _s and all attributes in the field definition are applied on this field.

To create a facet on our `author_s` field, we need to get the `facetset` component from the Solarium query, create a `facet field` key and set the actual field using the facets that will be created.

```
$query->setQuery('cat:book');
$facetset = $query->getFacetSet();
$facetset->createFacetField('author')->setField('author_s');
```

Set the number of facets to get using the following code:

```
$facetset->setLimit(5);
```

Return all facets that have at least one term in them.

```
$facetset->setMinCount(1);
```

Also return documents that do not have any value for the facet field.

```
$facetset->setMissing(true);
```

After executing the query, we will have to get the facets and counts by the facet field key.

```
$resultSet = $client->select($query);
$facetData = $resultSet->getFacetSet()->getFacet('author');
foreach($facetData as $item => $count)
{
  echo $item.": [".$count."] <br/>".PHP_EOL;
}
```

In addition, we can use the setOffset(int $offset) function to show faceting starting from this offset. The setOffset(int $offset) and setLimit(int $limit) functions can be used for pagination within facets.

On going through the Solr logs, we can see the query that was executed on Solr.

```
928567 [http-bio-8080-exec-9] INFO  org.apache.solr.core.SolrCore  -
[collection1] webapp=/solr path=/select params={omitHeader=true&facet.
missing=true&facet=true&fl=id,name,price,author,score,last_
modified&facet.mincount=1&start=0&q=cat:book&facet.limit=5&facet.
field={!key%3Dauthor}author_s&facet.field={!key%3Dgenre}
genre_s&wt=json&rows=25} hits=30 status=0 QTime=2
```

The parameter `facet=true` is passed to enable faceting. Fields on which we need faceting are passed as multiple `facet.field` values. Other parameters that we can see here are `facet.missing`, `facet.mincount`, and `facet.limit`. To check out the Solr response to facet query, let us copy the query from logs, paste it to our Solr URL, and remove the `omitHeaders` and `wt` parameters.

```
http://localhost:8080/solr/collection1/select/?facet.missing=true&
facet=true&fl=id,name,price,author,score,last_modified&facet.minco
unt=1&start=0&q=cat:book&facet.limit=5&facet.field={!key%3Dauthor}
author_s&facet.field={!key%3Dgenre}genre_s&rows=25
```

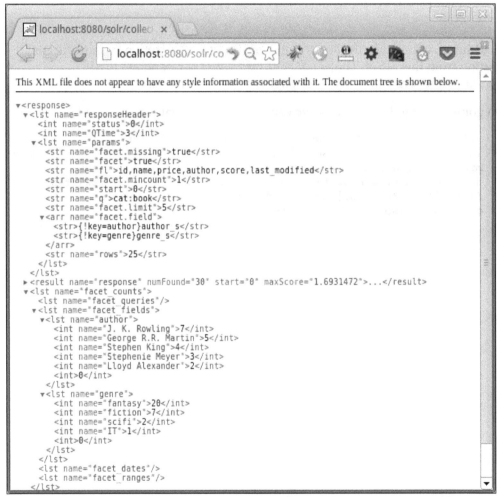

Facets are on fields – author and genre. Counts for different authors and genres are visible.

Facet by query

We can use a facet query in addition to the normal query to get counts with respect to the facet query. The counts are not affected by the main query and filter queries can be excluded from it. Let's see the code to get counts of facets where genre is fantasy and also see an example of excluding a filter query.

Let us first create a query to select all books in our index.

```
$query->setQuery('cat:book');
```

Create a filter query for books that are in stock and tag it.

```
$fquery = $query->createFilterQuery('inStock');
$fquery->setQuery('inStock:true');
$fquery->addTag('inStockTag');
```

Get the facetset component from our query using the following code:

```
$facetset = $query->getFacetSet();
```

Create a facet by query to count the number of books of a particular genre. Also, exclude the filter query we added earlier.

```
$facetqry = $facetset->createFacetQuery('genreFantasy');
$facetqry->setQuery('genre_s: fantasy');
$facetqry->addExclude('inStockTag');
```

Let us add another facet query where the filter query is not excluded:

```
$facetqry = $facetset->createFacetQuery('genreFiction');
$facetqry->setQuery('genre_s: fiction');
```

After the query is executed, we can get the count from the resultset.

```
$fantasyCnt = $resultSet->getFacetSet()->getFacet('genreFantasy')-
>getValue();
$fictionCnt = $resultSet->getFacetSet()->getFacet('genreFiction')-
>getValue();
```

Here the count for the fantasy facet contains books that are not in stock as well because we had excluded the filter query for getting books that are in stock. Whereas, the fiction facet contains only books that are in stock as the filter query has not been excluded in this facet query.

```
1973307 [http-bio-8080-exec-9] INFO  org.apache.solr.core.
SolrCore  - [collection1] webapp=/solr path=/select param
s={omitHeader=true&facet=true&fl=id,name,price,author,sco
re,last_modified&facet.query={!key%3DgenreFantasy+ex%3DinS
```

```
tockTag}genre_s:+fantasy&facet.query={!key%3DgenreFiction}
genre_s:+fiction&start=0&q=cat:book&wt=json&fq={!tag%3DinStockTag}
inStock:true&rows=25} hits=24 status=0 QTime=2
```

From Solr logs, we can see that the parameter being passed for creating facets using query is `facet.query`.

Facet counts for queries on genre fantasy and fiction

We can create multiple facet queries for getting counts of different query facets. But it is easier to use the **facet multiquery** feature provided by Solarium. Let us see the code to get facet counts for `genre` as `fantasy` and `fiction` using the facet multiquery feature:

```
$facetmqry = $facetset->createFacetMultiQuery('genre');
$facetmqry->createQuery('genre_fantasy','genre_s: fantasy');
$facetmqry->createQuery('genre_fiction','genre_s: fiction');
```

Here is the code to get the facet counts for all facet queries after executing the main query.

```
$facetCnts = $resultSet->getFacetSet()->getFacet('genre');
foreach($facetCnts as $fct => $cnt){
  echo $fct.': ['.$cnt.']'."<br/>".PHP_EOL;
}
```

The Solr query created using `facetMultiQuery` and `facetQuery` is the same.

Facet by range

Faceting can also be done on range basis. So for example, we can create facet counts of books for every two dollars. Using range faceting, we can give counts of books with prices between 0-2 dollars and from 2-4 dollars and so on.

```
$facetqry = $facetset->createFacetRange('pricerange');
$facetqry->setField('price');
$facetqry->setStart(0);
$facetqry->setGap(2);
$facetqry->setEnd(16);
```

In the preceding code, we start faceting from price 0 dollars and up to 16 dollars. The following code will be used to display the range facets along with their counts after executing the query:

```
$facetCnts = $resultSet->getFacetSet()->getFacet('pricerange');
foreach($facetCnts as $range => $cnt){
  echo $range.' to '.($range+2).': ['.$cnt.']'."<br/>".PHP_EOL;
}
```

Facet by range output

```
5481523 [http-bio-8080-exec-4] INFO  org.apache.solr.core.SolrCore  -
[collection1] webapp=/solr path=/select params={facet=true&f.price.
facet.range.gap=2&facet.range={!key%3Dpricerange+ex%3DinStockTag}pric
e&wt=json&rows=5&omitHeader=true&f.price.facet.range.other=all&fl=id,n
```

```
ame,price,author,score,last_modified&start=0&q=cat:book&f.price.facet.
range.end=16&fq={!tag%3DinStockTag}inStock:true&f.price.facet.range.
start=0} hits=24 status=0 QTime=29
```

The parameter used in the Solr query in this case is `facet.range`. It is possible to provide more than one faceting parameters together. For example, we can facet by query and facet by range in a single query.

Facet by pivot

In addition to the different ways of creating facets, there is a concept of **facet by pivots** that is provided by Solr and is exposed via Solarium. Pivot faceting allows us to create facets within the results of the parent facet. The input to pivot faceting is a set of fields to pivot on. Multiple fields create multiple sections in the response.

Here is the code to create a facet pivot on `genre` and `availability` (in stock):

```php
$facetqry = $facetset->createFacetPivot('genre-instock');
$facetqry->addFields('genre_s,inStock');
```

To display the pivots, we have to get all facets from the resultset.

```php
$facetResult = $resultSet->getFacetSet()->getFacet('genre-instock');
```

And for each facet, get the field, value, and count for the facet and more facet pivots within the facet.

```php
echo 'Field: '.$pivot->getField().PHP_EOL;
echo 'Value: '.$pivot->getValue().PHP_EOL;
echo 'Count: '.$pivot->getCount().PHP_EOL;
```

Also get all pivots inside this facet and process them in the same fashion using recursive calls if required.

```php
$pivot->getPivot();
```

This feature is very helpful in creating a complete categorization of data as facets at different levels. From Solr query logs it is seen that the parameter used here is `facet.pivot`.

```
6893766 [http-bio-8080-exec-10] INFO  org.apache.solr.core.SolrCore  -
[collection1] webapp=/solr path=/select params={omitHeader=true&face
t=true&fl=id,name,price,author,score,last_modified&start=0&q=cat:boo
k&facet.pivot.mincount=0&wt=json&facet.pivot=genre_s,inStock&rows=5}
hits=30 status=0 QTime=9
```

On executing the same query on the Solr interface, we get the following output.

```
http://localhost:8080/solr/collection1/select/?facet=true&fl=id,na
me,price,author,score,last_modified&start=0&q=cat:book&facet.pivot.
mincount=0&facet.pivot=genre_s,inStock&rows=5
```

```
▼<response>
 ▶<lst name="responseHeader">...</lst>
 ▶<result name="response" numFound="30" start="0" maxScore="1.6931472">...</result>
 ▼<lst name="facet_counts">
    <lst name="facet_queries"/>
    <lst name="facet_fields"/>
    <lst name="facet_dates"/>
    <lst name="facet_ranges"/>
   ▼<lst name="facet_pivot">
     ▼<arr name="genre_s,inStock">
       ▼<lst>
          <str name="field">genre_s</str>
          <str name="value">fantasy</str>
          <int name="count">20</int>
         ▼<arr name="pivot">
           ▼<lst>
              <str name="field">inStock</str>
              <bool name="value">true</bool>
              <int name="count">18</int>
            </lst>
           ▼<lst>
              <str name="field">inStock</str>
              <bool name="value">false</bool>
              <int name="count">2</int>
            </lst>
          </arr>
        </lst>
       ▼<lst>
          <str name="field">genre_s</str>
          <str name="value">fiction</str>
          <int name="count">7</int>
         ▼<arr name="pivot">
           ▼<lst>
              <str name="field">inStock</str>
              <bool name="value">false</bool>
              <int name="count">4</int>
            </lst>
           ▼<lst>
              <str name="field">inStock</str>
              <bool name="value">true</bool>
              <int name="count">3</int>
            </lst>
          </arr>
        </lst>
       ▼<lst>
```

The first level of categorization happens on the genre field. Inside the genre, the second level of categorization happens on the inStock field.

Summary

In this chapter, we saw advanced query functionalities of Solr. We defined filter queries and saw the benefits of using filter queries instead of normal queries. We saw how to do faceting on Solr using PHP and Solarium. We saw different ways to facet results as facets by field, facets by query, facets by range and creating facet pivots. We also saw the actual queries being executed on Solr and in some cases executed the query on Solr and saw the results.

In the next chapter, we will explore highlighting of search results using PHP and Solr.

5

Highlighting Results Using PHP and Solr

One of the advanced functionalities that Solr provides is highlighting the matched keywords in the results returned for a search. In addition to the highlighted matches, it is also possible to specify the number of highlighted snippets that we want Solr to return per field. In this chapter, we will be exploring all the highlighting functionalities of Solr using PHP and the Solarium library. The topics that we will cover are:

- Solr highlighting configuration
- Highlighting in Solr using PHP and Solarium
- Using different highlighting tags for different fields
- Highlighting using the fast vector highlighter

 The field on which highlighting is required has to be stored in Solr.

Solr highlighting configuration

Solr has two types of highlighters—**regular highlighter** and **fast vector highlighter**. The regular highlighter works on most query types but does not scale well to large documents. On the other hand, the fast vector highlighter scales very well to large documents but supports fewer query types. Though personally I have not come across a situation where the fast vector highlighter does not work.

The fast vector highlighter requires `termVectors`, `termPositions`, and `termOffsets` to be set for it to work.

Let us look at the Solr configuration for highlighting. Open up the Solr configuration at `<solr_directory>/example/solr/collection1/conf/solrconfig.xml`. Search for an XML element `searchComponent` with attribute `class="solr.HighlightComponent"` and `name="highlight"`. We can see that there are multiple **fragmenters**, an HTML **formatter**, and an HTML **encoder** defined in the file. We also have multiple `fragmentsBuilders`, multiple `fragListBuilders` and multiple `boundaryScanners` defined as explained in the following list:

- **Fragmenter:** It is the text snippet generator for highlighted text. The default fragmenter is a gap that is marked by `default="true"`.

- **Formatter**: It is used to format the output and specifies the HTML tags to be used to highlight the output. The tags are customizable and can be passed in the URL.

- **fragListBuilder:** It is used with `FastVectorHighlighter` only. It is used to define the size (in characters) of snippets created by the highlighter for `FastVectorHighlighter`. The default `fragListBuilder` is `single`, which can be used to indicate that the whole field should be used without any fragmenting.

- **fragmentsBuilder**: It is used with `FastVectorHighlighter` to specify tags to be used for highlighting. It can be overwritten by using `hl.tag.pre` and `hl.tag.post` parameters.

- **boundaryScanner**: It defines how boundaries are determined for `FastVectorHighlighter` only. The default `boundaryScanner` defines the boundary characters as `.,!?\t\n` and space.

 More details about highlighting parameters can be obtained from the following URL : `https://cwiki.apache.org/confluence/display/solr/Standard+Highlighter`

Highlighting in Solr using PHP and Solarium

Let us try regular highlighting using PHP. Search for harry in our index and highlight two fields — name and series_t as shown in the following code:

```
$query->setQuery('harry');
$query->setFields(array
    ('id','name','author','series_t','score','last_modified'));
```

First get the highlighting component from the following query:

```
$hl = $query->getHighlighting();
```

Set fields we want to highlight using the following query:

```
$hl->setFields('name,series_t');
```

Set the highlighting HTML tags as bold using the following query:

```
$hl->setSimplePrefix('<strong>');
$hl->setSimplePostfix('</strong>');
```

Set the maximum number of highlighted snippets to be generated per field. In this case any number of highlighted snippets from 0 to 2 can be generated as shown in the following query:

```
$hl->setSnippets(2);
```

Set the size in characters of fragments to consider for highlighting. 0 uses the whole field value without any fragmentation as shown in the following query:

```
$hl->setFragSize(0);
```

Set the mergeContiguous flag to merge contiguous fragments into a single fragment as shown in the following code:

```
$hl->setMergeContiguous(true);
```

Set highlightMultiTerm flag to enable highlighting for range, wildcard, fuzzy, and prefix queries as shown in the following query:

```
$hl->setHighlightMultiTerm(true);
```

Once the query is run and the result-set is received, we will need to retrieve the highlighted results from the result-set with the following query:

```
$hlresults = $resultSet->getHighlighting();
```

For each document in the result-set, we will need to get the highlighted document from the highlighted result-set. We will need to pass the unique ID as identifier in the `getResult()` function to get the highlighted document as shown in the following code:

```
foreach($resultSet as $doc)
{
  $hldoc = $hlresults->getResult($doc->id);
  $hlname = implode(',',$hldoc->getField('name'));
  $hlseries = implode(',',$hldoc->getField('series_t'));
}
```

Here the highlighted fields for each document, which we obtain using the `getField()` method, function is returned as an array. This is why we have to implode it before display. We can see that in the output the fields are highlighted using the bold—`<strong>` and `</strong>` tags.

In Solr logs, we can see all the parameters that we have specified in our PHP code as given in the following:

```
336647163 [http-bio-8080-exec-1] INFO
  org.apache.solr.core.SolrCore  - [collection1] webapp=/solr
  path=/select params=
  {hl.fragsize=0&hl.mergeContiguous=true&hl.simple.pre=
  <strong>&hl.fl=name,series_t&wt=json&hl=true
  &rows=25&hl.highlightMultiTerm=true&omitHeader=true
  &fl=id,name,author,series_t,score,last_modified
  &hl.snippets=2&start=0&q=harry&hl.simple.post=</strong>}
  hits=7 status=0 QTime=203
```

The parameter passed to enable highlighting is `hl=true` and the fields to be highlighted is specified as `hl.fl=name,series_t`.

Using different highlighting tags for different fields

We can use different highlighting tags for different fields. Let us highlight `name` with a `bold` tag and `series` with an `italics` tag. Set the `per` field tag in our code as shown in the following:

```
$hl->getField('name')->setSimplePrefix('<strong>')-
  >setSimplePostfix('</strong>');
$hl->getField('series_t')->setSimplePrefix('<em>')-
  >setSimplePostfix('</em>');
```

The output shows that field `name` is highlighted with a bold tag whereas the field `series` is highlighted with an italics tag as shown in the following screenshot:

id	name	author	series	score
043932162X	**Harry** potter and The Philosopherâ€™s Stone	J. K. Rowling	The *Harry* Potter Collection	0.952404
id	name	author	series	score
1408812575	**Harry** Potter And The Deathly Hallows	J. K. Rowling	The *Harry* Potter Collection	0.952404
id	name	author	series	score
1408812525	**Harry** Potter And The Chamber Of Secrets	J. K. Rowling	The *Harry* Potter Collection	0.7619232
id	name	author	series	score
1408812535	**Harry** Potter And The Prisoner Of Azkaban	J. K. Rowling	The *Harry* Potter Collection	0.7619232
id	name	author	series	score
1408812545	**Harry** Potter And The Goblet Of Fire	J. K. Rowling	The *Harry* Potter Collection	0.7619232

Highlighting different fields with different tags.

We can also use the `setQuery()` function to set a separate query for highlighting results other than the normal query. In the earlier program, let us change the highlighting to happen on `harry potter` on the search for `harry` as shown in the following code:

```
$hl->setQuery('harry potter');
```

On checking Solr logs it is seen that the query to be used for highlighting is passed as `hl.q` parameter to Solr as shown in the following code:

```
344378867 [http-bio-8080-exec-9] INFO
  org.apache.solr.core.SolrCore  - [collection1] webapp=/solr
  path=/select params={f.series_t.hl.simple.pre=<i>&f.name.
  hl.simple.post=</b>&f.name.hl.simple.pre=<b>&hl.
  fl=name,series_t&wt=json&hl=true&rows=25
  &omitHeader=true&hl.highlightMultiTerm=true
  &fl=id,name,author,series_t,score,last_modified
  &f.series_t.hl.simple.post=</i>&hl.snippets=2
  &start=0&q=harry&hl.q=harry+potter} hits=7 status=0 QTime=27
```

Highlighting using the fast vector highlighter

Let us change the schema.xml and enable **termVectors**, **termPositions**, and **termOffsets** for two fields name and *_t (this will match all fields ending with _t-series_t).

```
<field name="name" type="text_general" indexed="true"
  stored="true" termVectors="true" termPositions="true"
 termOffsets="true"/>
<dynamicField name="*_t"  type="text_general" indexed="true"
  stored="true" termVectors="true" termPositions="true"
  termOffsets="true"/>
```

Restart Tomcat. Based on your system (Windows or Linux) and the type of installation, the mechanism to restart Tomcat will differ. Kindly check the Tomcat documentation for your system to restart Tomcat.

Since the schema is now changed, we will need to re-index all the documents that we had indexed in *Chapter 2, Inserting, Updating and Deleting Documents from Solr*. Also index the books.csv file from this chapter. In code, enable fast highlighting and set the fragmentsBuilder (HTML tags) to be used for highlighting as shown in the following queries:

```
$hl->setUseFastVectorHighlighter(true);
$hl->setFragmentsBuilder('colored');
```

In the output we can see that harry is highlighted. To change the default highlighting, we need to add a new **fragmentsBuilder** in the solrconfig.xml file. Go through the solrconfig.xml file and search for the tag fragmentsBuilder with the name colored. This has two attributes—hl.tag.pre and hl.tag.post. We can specify the pre and post tags for fast vector highlighting here. Create a new fragmentsbuilder after it with the name fasthl as shown in the following code:

```
<fragmentsBuilder name="fasthl"
  class="solr.highlight.ScoreOrderFragmentsBuilder">
<lst name="defaults">
<str name="hl.tag.pre"><![CDATA[<b
  style="background:cyan">]]></str>
<str name="hl.tag.post"><![CDATA[</b>]]></str>
</lst>
</fragmentsBuilder>
```

Restart Tomcat and change the PHP code to use this new fragmentbuilder for highlighting as given in the following query:

```
$hl->setFragmentsBuilder('fasthl');
```

The output now will contain `harry` highlighted in a light blue color.

It is also possible to change the highlighting tags at runtime using `setTagPrefix()` and `setTagPostfix()` function. In the following code, we are changing the tags for fast vector highlighting to lime colored in our code:

```
$hl->setTagPrefix('<b style="background:lime">')-
    >setTagPostfix('</b>');
```

The configuration file is used to set default highlighting tags. And the tags can be changed at runtime using PHP function calls for formatting purposes.

Here are some additional functions available in Solarium that can be used to suit highlighting to your requirements:

- `setUsePhraseHighlighter(boolean $use)`: Set `true` to highlight phrase terms only when they appear within the query phrase in a document. Default is `true`.

- `setRequireFieldMatch(boolean $require)`: Set `true` to highlight a field only if the query matched in this particular field. By default this is false and so terms are highlighted in all requested fields regardless of which field matched the query. Requires `setUsePhraseHighlighter(true)`.

- `setRegexPattern(string $pattern)`: It is used in regular highlighter only. Used to set regular expression for fragmenting.

- `setAlternateField(string $field)`: If none of the terms match and no snippet could be generated, we can set an alternate/fallback field to be used to generate snippets.

- `setMaxAlternateFieldLength(int $length)`: It is used only when the alternate field is set. It specifies the maximum number of characters of the alternate field to return. The default is `unlimited`.

Summary

We saw how to ask Solr for highlighted search results using PHP code. We saw the regular and fastvector highlighter. We saw the functions and parameters used to change the highlighting tags for both regular and fastvector highlighter. We also went through some functions and Solr configuration and schema changes to tweak highlighting and the generated snippets.

In the next chapter, we will go in depth on the scoring mechanism. We will explore the debug and stats component, which will enable us to improve relevance ranking and get statistics information from the index respectively.

6
Debug and Stats Component

Debug and stats are two components in Solarium used to get more information about the index statistics and how queries are executed and results returned. In this chapter we will explore both the components and go in depth on how to retrieve the index statistics using the stats component. We will also look at how Solr calculates relevance scores and how we can use PHP to get and display the query explanation returned by Solr. We will explore:

- How Solr does relevance ranking
- Executing a debug through PHP code
- Running a debug on Solr interface
- Displaying the output of debug query
- Display query result statistics using the stats component

You could say why should I go into the theory about these components? What will this help me achieve? The benefit of using the debug component is to understand and analyze how the search result was ranked. Why did a certain document come on the top and why did another document come at the end? Further if you want to alter the ranking to suit the way you want results to be displayed, you have to boost certain fields and again debug and analyze how the query is performing after applying the boosts. In a single line, the debug component helps us in analyzing and modifying the ranking to suit our requirements. The stats component is mostly used for displaying index statistics—something that can be used to show the complexity of the index being handled.

Solr relevance ranking

When a query is passed to Solr, it is converted to an appropriate query string that is then executed by Solr. For each document in the result, Solr calculates the relevance score according to which the document is sorted. By default higher scoring documents are given priority in the result.

The Solr relevancy algorithm is known as the **tf-idf model** where **tf** stands for **term frequency** and **idf** stands for **inverse document frequency**. The meaning of the parameters used in relevance calculation so we can interpret the output of debug query are explained as follows:

- **tf**: The term frequency is the frequency with which a term appears in a document. Higher term frequency results in a high document score.

- **idf**: The inverse document frequency is the inverse of the number of documents in which the term appears. It indicates the rarity of the term across all documents in the index. Documents having a rare term are scored higher.

- **coord**: It is the coordination factor that says how many query terms were found in a document. A document with more query terms will have higher score.

- **queryNorm**: It is a normalizing factor used to make the scores across queries comparable. Since all documents are multiplied by the same queryNorm, it does not affect the document ranking.

- **fieldNorm**: Field normalization penalizes fields with a large number of terms. If a field contains more terms than the other, its score is lower than the other.

We have seen query time boosts earlier. The purpose of debugging a query is to see how relevance is being calculated and use our knowledge of query time boosts to tune the output as per our requirement.

Executing debug through PHP code

To enable debugging of our Solr query using PHP, we need to get the debug component from our query.

In addition to getting debug information of the default query, we can call the `explainOther()` function to get a score of certain documents that match the query specified in `explainOther()` function with respect to the main query as shown in the following query:

```
$query->setQuery('cat:book OR author:martin^2');
$debugq = $query->getDebug();
$debugq->setExplainOther('author:king');
```

In the preceding piece of code, we are searching for all books and boosting books by author martin by 2. In addition to this we are getting the debug information for books by author king.

After running the query, we need to get the debug component from the ResultSet. We then use it to get the query string, parsed query string, the query parser and information about the debug other query as shown in the following code:

```
echo 'Querystring: ' . $dResultSet->getQueryString() . '<br/>';
echo 'Parsed query: ' . $dResultSet->getParsedQuery() . '<br/>';
echo 'Query parser: ' . $dResultSet->getQueryParser() . '<br/>';
echo 'Other query: ' . $dResultSet->getOtherQuery() . '<br/>';
```

We need to iterate over the debug result-set and for each document we need to get the total score value, the match and the score calculation description. We can also get into the details of the debug information and obtain the value, match, and calculation description for each term in the query with respect to the document as shown in the following code:

```
foreach ($dResultSet->getExplain() as $key => $explanation) {
echo '<h3>Document key: ' . $key . '</h3>';
echo 'Value: ' . $explanation->getValue() . '<br/>';
echo 'Match: ' . (($explanation->getMatch() == true) ? 'true' :
  'false')  . '<br/>';
echo 'Description: ' . $explanation->getDescription() . '<br/>';
echo '<h4>Details</h4>';
foreach ($explanation as $detail) {
echo 'Value: ' . $detail->getValue() . '<br/>';
echo 'Match: ' . (($detail->getMatch() == true) ? 'true' :
  'false')  . '<br/>';
echo 'Description: ' . $detail->getDescription() . '<br/>';
echo '<hr/>';
}
}
```

To obtain the debug information for the other query we need to call the getExplainOther() function and follow the same process as above. In addition to the scoring information, we also get the time taken for each phase of query execution. This can be obtained by using the getTiming() function as below.

```
echo 'Total time: ' . $dResultSet->getTiming()->getTime() .
  '<br/>';
```

To obtain the time spent in each phase of the query, we need to iterate over the output of the `getPhases()` function and get the phase name related data.

```
foreach ($dResultSet->getTiming()->getPhases() as $phaseName =>
  $phaseData) {
echo '<h4>' . $phaseName . '</h4>';
foreach ($phaseData as $subType => $time) {
echo $subType . ': ' . $time . '<br/>';
}
}
```

Running debug on Solr interface

The parameters appended to the Solr query URL in our example are `debugQuery=true`, `explainOther=author:king`, and `debug.explain.structured=true`. Let us check the Solr output for a debug query by visiting the URL `http://localhost:8080/solr/collection1/select/?omitHeader=true&debugQuery=true&fl=id,name,author,series_t,score,price&start=0&q=cat:book+OR+author:martin^2&rows=5`

The following is a screenshot of the output of the previous query:

We can see the debug component after the results component in Solr query results interface. It contains the raw query and parsed query. The explain element in the debug component contains the score and the calculations that were done to achieve the score

Since debugging a Solr query is required to tune the relevance, it makes more sense to use the Solr interface to see the debug output. PHP interface to the debug component can be used to create an interactive user interface where field level boosts are taken from the user and used to calculate and display the relevance. Such an interface can be used to see how changes in boost affect the relevance score and tune the same.

The stats component

The stats component can be used to return simple statistics for indexed numeric fields in the document set returned by a Solr query. Let us get the statistics for prices of all books in our index. We will also facet on price and availability (inStock) and see the output.

 It is advisable to use a templating engine instead of writing HTML code inside PHP.

Create the query to fetch all books and set the number of rows to 0 as we are not interested in the results but only the statistics, which will be fetched as a separate component as given in the following query:

```
$query->setQuery('cat:book');
$query->setRows(0);
```

Get the stats component and create statistics for field price and create facets on price and inStock fields.

```
$statsq = $query->getStats();
$statsq->createField('price')->addFacet('price')-
  >addFacet('inStock');
```

Execute the query and fetch the stats component from the result-set as given in the following query:

```
$resultset = $client->select($query);
$statsResult = $resultset->getStats();
```

Loop through the fields we have fetched in our stats component earlier. Get all statistics for each field as shown in the following code:

```
foreach($statsResult as $field) {
echo '<b>Statistics for '.$field->getName().'</b><br/>';
echo 'Min: ' . $field->getMin() . '<br/>';
echo 'Max: ' . $field->getMax() . '<br/>';
echo 'Sum: ' . $field->getSum() . '<br/>';
echo 'Count: ' . $field->getCount() . '<br/>';
echo 'Missing: ' . $field->getMissing() . '<br/>';
echo 'SumOfSquares: ' . $field->getSumOfSquares() . '<br/>';
echo 'Mean: ' . $field->getMean() . '<br/>';
echo 'Stddev: ' . $field->getStddev() . '<br/>';
```

Get the facets for each field in the statistics result-set and fetch the statistics for each element in the facet results as shown in the following code:

```
foreach ($field->getFacets() as $fld => $fct) {
echo '<hr/><b>Facet for '.$fld.'</b><br/>';
foreach ($fct as $fctStats) {
echo '<b>' . $fld . ' = ' . $fctStats->getValue() . '</b><br/>';
echo 'Min: ' . $fctStats->getMin() . '<br/>';
echo 'Max: ' . $fctStats->getMax() . '<br/>';
echo 'Sum: ' . $fctStats->getSum() . '<br/>';
echo 'Count: ' . $fctStats->getCount() . '<br/>';
echo 'Missing: ' . $fctStats->getMissing() . '<br/>';
echo 'SumOfSquares: ' . $fctStats->getSumOfSquares() . '<br/>';
echo 'Mean: ' . $fctStats->getMean() . '<br/>';
echo 'Stddev: ' . $fctStats->getStddev() . '<br/><br/>';
}
}
```

The output of our script can be seen in the following screenshot:

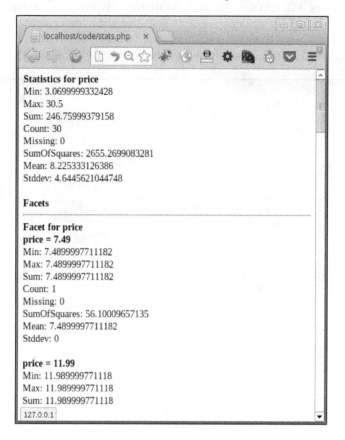

On checking Solr logs we can see the query being executed as follows:

```
4105213 [http-bio-8080-exec-2] INFO
   org.apache.solr.core.SolrCore  - [collection1] webapp=/solr
   path=/select params={omitHeader=true&fl=*,score&start=0
   &stats.field=price&stats=true&q=cat:book
   &f.price.stats.facet=price&f.price.stats.
   facet=inStock&wt=json&rows=0} hits=30 status=0 QTime=7
```

To enable statistics, we have to pass `stats=true` along with `stats.field` and faceting parameters. We can see the same statistics output on Solr using the URL `http://localhost:8080/solr/collection1/select/?omitHeader=true&rows=0 &stats.field=price&stats=true&q=cat:book&f.price.stats.facet=price&f. price.stats.facet=inStock` as shown in the following screenshot:

In the preceding screenshot we can see the statistics for **price** and statistics facets for **price** and **inStock**. Out of our complete stock of books, the minimum price is **3.06** and the maximum price is **30.5**. The sum of all prices is **246.76** and the mean is **8.225**. We can see similar information for each element in our facet output.

Summary

This chapter gave us some insight into our index and into how results are ranked. We saw the parameters used to calculate the relevance score and how to extract the calculation from Solr using PHP. We discussed the use of the debug query. We saw how to extract statistics of numeric fields for a query from our index and how to display the information using PHP. The information retrieved from these modules is used to analyze and improve the Solr search results. Statistics can also be used for reporting purposes.

In the next chapter we will explore how to build spell suggestions using the Solr and PHP. We will also build an auto complete feature to suggest query options during a search.

7
Spell Check in Solr

The spell check component can be used to suggest spelling corrections based on the data we have in our index. In this chapter, we will see how to enable spell check in our index and use PHP to get and display spelling corrections. The topics that we will cover in this chapter are as follows:

- Solr configuration for spell check
- Spell checker implementations available in Solr
- Running a spell check query using PHP
- Displaying suggestions and collations
- Building the autocomplete feature

 Spell check works on indexed words. If our index has incorrect spellings, the suggestions may also be misspelled.

Spell check can be used to suggest spelling corrections to the user by providing a *did you mean* functionality. It is similar to the **showing results for** feature that Google provides. It can be used to provide a list of suggestions for autocompleting the user's input text. PHP also has a similar functionality known as **pspell** but this spellcheck is built on top of the index that we have created in Solr. This means that it is more customized to the type of documents that are there in the index and also can be tweaked for results that are more to our liking.

Solr configuration for spell check

The demo schema and configuration that comes with Solr installation already has spell check configured in it. Let us look at its settings:

1. Open up `solrconfig.xml` inside `<solr_dir>/example/solr/collection1/conf`.

2. Search for `searchComponent` by the name of `spellcheck`.

3. Inside the `spellcheck` component there are multiple spellchecker(s). Here is the `default` spellchecker that comes along with Solr:

```
<lst name="spellchecker">
<str name="name">default</str>
<str name="field">text</str>
<str name="classname">solr.DirectSolrSpellChecker</str>
<float name="accuracy">0.5</float>
<int name="maxEdits">2</int>
<int name="minPrefix">1</int>
<int name="maxInspections">5</int>
<int name="minQueryLength">4</int>
<float name="maxQueryFrequency">0.01</float>
<float name="thresholdTokenFrequency">.01</float>
</lst>
```

4. The preceding block of code shows various variables used in spell check. Let us go through the important variables in spell check configuration and check out their meanings:

   - `name`: This variable specifies the name of the spell check configuration of the Solr spellchecker. In our configuration the name is `default`.

   - `field`: This variable specifies the field that will be used for spellchecking. We are using the text field to load tokens for spellchecking.

   - `classname`: This variable specifies the implementation of Solr spellchecker that is being used. We are using `DirectSolrSpellChecker`, which uses the Solr index directly and does not require us to build or rebuild the spell check index. We will look at other implementations as well.

   - `accuracy`: This variable ranges from `0.0` to `1.0`, `1.0` being most accurate. This accuracy value is used by the Solr spell checking implementation to decide if the results can be used or not.

- ° `maxQueryFrequency`: This variable specifies the maximum threshold for the number of documents a query term must appear in to be considered as a suggestion. Here it is set to `0.01`. A lower threshold is better for smaller indexes.

- ° `thresholdTokenFrequency`: This variable specifies that the term must occur in one percent of the documents to be considered for spelling suggestions. This prevents low frequency terms from being offered as suggestions. But if your document base is small, you may need to reduce this further to get spelling suggestions.

Spell checker implementations available with Solr

Let us go through the different spell checker implementations available with Solr:

- `DirectSolrSpellChecker`: This implementation does not require a separate index to be built for spell checking. It uses the main Solr index for spelling suggestions.

- `IndexBasedSpellChecker`: This implementation is used to create and maintain a spelling dictionary that is based on the Solr index. Since a separate index is created and maintained, we need to build/rebuild the index whenever the main index changes. This can be done automatically by enabling `buildOnCommit` or `buildOnOptimize` in the configuration. Also, we need to specify the location of the index to be created using the `spellcheckIndexDir` variable in our Solr spellcheck component configuration.

> The `buildOnCommit` component is very expensive. It is recommended to use `buildOnOptimize` or explicit build using `spellcheck.build=true` in Solr URL.

- `FileBasedSpellChecker`: This implementation uses a flat file to build a spellcheck index in Solr. Since there is no frequency information available, the index created using this component cannot be used to extract frequency based information such as threshold or most popular suggestions. The format of the file is one word per line, for example:

```
Java
PHP
MySQL
Solr
```

The index needs to be built using the `spellcheck.build=true` parameter in our Solr URL. In addition to the `spellcheckIndexDir` location to build and store the index, the `FileBasedSpellChecker` component also needs the `sourceLocation` variable to specify the location of the spelling file.

- `WordBreakSolrSpellChecker`: This spellcheck component generates suggestions by combining adjacent words or by breaking words into multiples. It can be configured along with one of the preceding spellcheckers. In this case, the results are combined and collations can contain a result from both spellcheckers.

Spellcheckers generally give suggestions that are sorted by the score from the string distance calculation and then by frequency of suggestions in the index. These parameters can be tuned in the configuration file by providing different implementations of the distance calculation using the `distanceMeasure` variable or by providing different implementations of word frequency using the `comparatorClass` variable. Some available `comparatorClass` implementations are `score` (default) and `freq`. Similarly `org.apache.lucene.search.spell.JaroWinklerDistance` is an implementation of distance calculation, which is available with Solr.

Running a spell check query using PHP

Let us configure Solr so that spell check happens on two fields, name and author:

1. Change the contents of the `schema.xml` file. Create a new field on which spellcheck will happen and copy the `name` and `author` fields to the new field using the following code:

   ```
   <field name="spellfld" type="text_general" indexed="true"
   stored="false" multiValued="true"/>
   <copyField source="name" dest="spellfld"/>
   <copyField source="author" dest="spellfld"/>
   ```

2. Change the spellchecker field for the default spellchecker in `solrconfig.xml` to the new field we have just created. The default spellchecker uses the `DirectSolrSpellChecker` implementation of spell checker available with Solr.

   ```
   <lst name="spellchecker">
   <str name="name">default</str>
   <str name="field">spellfld</str>
   ```

3. By default the `/select` request handler in Solr configuration does not have spellcheck settings and results. So let us add these variables in `requestHandler` named `/select`. Here we are specifying the spellcheck dictionary to be used as **default**, which we configured earlier and adding the spell check component as a part of the output.

```
<requestHandler name="/select" class="solr.SearchHandler">
<lst name="defaults">
.....
<!-- spell check settings -->
<str name="spellcheck.dictionary">default</str>
<str name="spellcheck">on</str>
</lst>

<arr name="last-components">
<str>spellcheck</str>
</arr>
```

4. Now restart Solr and reindex the `books.csv` file in the `exampledocs` folder and also the `books.csv` file provided in *Chapter 5, Highlighting Results Using PHP and Solr*. The reason why we need to index our books again is because we have changed our schema. Whenever schema is changed and new fields are added, the documents need to be indexed again to populate data in the new fields. Refer to the *Adding sample documents to Solr index* section in *Chapter 2, Inserting, Updating, and Deleting Documents from Solr*, for indexing these CSV files in Solr.

Let us do a spell check for the author *Stephen King* using PHP and see the corrections that Solr suggests:

1. First get the spell check component from the select query using the following code:

```
$spellChk = $query->getSpellcheck();
$spellChk->setCount(10);
$spellChk->setCollate(true);
$spellChk->setExtendedResults(true);
$spellChk->setCollateExtendedResults(true);
```

2. We have set the number of suggestions to return via the `setCount()` function. By setting `setCollate()` as `true`, we are telling Solr to suggest the original query string with best suggestions replacing the original misspelled words. The `setExtendedResults()` and `setCollateExtendedResults()` functions tell Solr to provide additional information about the suggestion and the collations returned. This can be used for analysis if required.

3. After executing the query, we need to get the spellcheck component from the query resultset and use it for getting suggestions and collations. We use the `getCorrectlySpelled()` function to check if the query was correctly spelled.

```
$resultset = $client->select($query);
$spellChkResult = $resultset->getSpellcheck();
if ($spellChkResult->getCorrectlySpelled()) {
echo 'yes';
}else{
echo 'no';
}
```

4. Next, we loop through the spellcheck results and for each term in the query we get the suggestions and related details such as number of suggestions, frequency of original term, and the suggested words with their frequency of occurrence.

```
foreach($spellChkResult as $suggestion) {
echo 'NumFound: '.$suggestion->getNumFound().'<br/>';
echo 'OriginalFrequency: '.$suggestion->getOriginalFrequency().'<
br/>';
foreach ($suggestion->getWords() as $word) {
echo 'Frequency: '.$word['freq'].'<br/>';
echo 'Word: '.$word['word'].'<br/>';
}
}
```

5. Similarly, we get the collations and loop through it to get the corrected query and hits. We can also get the details of corrections for each term in the query.

```
$collations = $spellChkResult->getCollations();
echo '<h1>Collations</h1>';
foreach($collations as $collation) {
echo 'Query: '.$collation->getQuery().'<br/>';
echo 'Hits: '.$collation->getHits().'<br/>';
foreach($collation->getCorrections() as $input => $correction) {
echo $input . ' => ' . $correction .'<br/>';
}
}
```

Implementing the autocomplete feature using PHP and Solr

Autocomplete feature can be built by creating a Suggester in Solr and using the Suggester available in Solarium. The purpose of autocomplete is to suggest query terms based on incomplete user input. Suggester works very similarly to the spellcheck feature. It can be made to work either on the main index or any other dictionary.

First let us change the schema.xml file to add a spellcheck component named suggest:

```
<searchComponent name="suggest" class="solr.SpellCheckComponent">
<lst name="spellchecker">
<str name="name">suggest</str>
<str name="field">suggestfld</str>
<str name="classname">org.apache.solr.spelling.suggest.Suggester</str>
<str name="lookupImpl">org.apache.solr.spelling.suggest.tst.
TSTLookup</str>
<str name="storeDir">suggest_idx</str>
<float name="threshold">0.005</float>
<str name="buildOnCommit">true</str>
</lst>
</searchComponent>
```

We have specified the field to use for suggestions as suggestfld. The Solr component that is used to build the Suggester is mentioned in the classname as org.apache.solr.spelling.suggest.Suggester. The threshold is a value between 0 and 1 that specifies the minimum fraction of documents where the term should appear to be added to the lookup dictionary. We are storing the index in the suggest_idx folder. The lookupImpl component provides the inmemory lookup implementations for creating suggestions. Available lookup implementations in Solr are:

- JaspellLookup: It is a tree-based representation based on Jaspell. Jaspell is a Java spelling checking package that creates a complex tree based structure for spelling corrections. It uses a data structure called trie.

- TSTLookup: It is a simple and compact ternary tree based representation, capable of immediate data structure updates. It also uses the trie data structure.

- FSTLookup: It is an automaton based representation. It is slower to build, but consumes far less memory at runtime.

- WFSTLookup: It is weighted automaton representation and an alternative to FSTLookup for more fine-grained ranking.

You can change the lookup implementations and check out how the suggestions change. Since the suggestions are based out of index, the larger the index is, the better the suggestions are.

Let us create a separate request handler in Solr for suggestions and add our suggest spellcheck as a component in it. The default configuration options for providing suggestions are incorporated in the request handler itself.

```
<requestHandler class="org.apache.solr.handler.component.
SearchHandler" name="/suggest">
<lst name="defaults">
<str name="spellcheck">true</str>
<str name="spellcheck.dictionary">suggest</str>
<str name="spellcheck.onlyMorePopular">true</str>
<str name="spellcheck.count">5</str>
<str name="spellcheck.collate">true</str>
</lst>
<arr name="components">
<str>suggest</str>
</arr>
</requestHandler>
```

Next, we will need to create a separate field in our schema.xml which is indexed. We are copying the book name, author, and title into the field to provide suggestions on them.

```
<field name="suggestfld" type="text_general" indexed="true"
stored="false" multiValued="false"/>

<copyField source="name" dest="suggestfld"/>
<copyField source="author" dest="suggestfld"/>
<copyField source="title" dest="suggestfld"/>
```

Once this is done, restart the Apache Tomcat web server and build the spellcheck index using the following URL:

```
http://localhost:8080/solr/collection1/suggest/?spellcheck.build=true
```

> We created a separate request handler named suggest, so our URL has / suggest/ instead of /select/.

Now let's go see the Suggester provided by the Solarium library for integration with PHP. First, we need to create a Suggester query from the Solarium client instead of the normal query.

```php
$client = new Solarium\Client($config);
$suggestqry = $client->createSuggester();
```

Next we have to set the request handler to use. Remember, we created a separate request handler named **suggest** to provide suggestions. Also set the dictionary we want to use. We can create multiple dictionaries and change them at runtime using the following functions:

```php
$suggestqry->setHandler('suggest');
$suggestqry->setDictionary('suggest');
```

Now provide the query for the Suggester. Set the number of suggestions to return. Turn on the `collation` flag and the `onlyMorePopular` flag.

```php
$suggestqry->setQuery('ste');
$suggestqry->setCount(5);
$suggestqry->setCollate(true);
$suggestqry->setOnlyMorePopular(true);
```

Execute the query using the `suggester()` function and then loop through the resultset to get all the terms and their suggestions. The original query can be displayed using the `getQuery()` function.

```php
$resultset = $client->suggester($suggestqry);
echo "Query : ".$suggestqry->getQuery();
foreach ($resultset as $term => $termResult) {
    echo '<strong>' . $term . '</strong><br/>';
    echo 'Suggestions:<br/>';
    foreach($termResult as $result){
        echo '-> '.$result.'<br/>';
    }
}
```

Finally, get and display the collations using the following code:

```php
echo 'Collation: '.$resultset->getCollation();
```

This piece of code can be used to create an AJAX call and provide autocomplete suggestions as a JSON or XML string.

Summary

We started with an understanding of how spell check works on Solr. We went through the configuration of Solr for creating spell check index and saw different implementations of the spellchecker available with Solr. We understood some of the fine tuning options available in spell check in Solr. Next, we created a field in Solr for doing spell check on book name and author and configured Solr to provide spelling suggestions using this field. We saw a variation of spell check that can be used to provide spelling suggestions for autocompletion. We created a separate Solr index for autocomplete suggestions and saw PHP code that takes a three-character word and provides suggestions from the index.

8

Advanced Solr – Grouping, the MoreLikeThis Query, and Distributed Search

In this chapter we will look at some of the advanced concepts of Solr. We will look at grouping results based on certain criteria. We will also look at finding results similar to a particular document based on some terms within the document. We will explore distributed search that can be used to horizontally scale the Solr search infrastructure. Topics that will be covered in this chapter are

- Grouping results by field
- Grouping results by query
- Running morelikethis query using PHP
- Tuning parameters of morelikethis query
- Distributed search
- Setting up distributed search
- Executing distributed search using PHP
- Setting up Solr master-slave
- Load balancing Solr queries using PHP

Grouping results by fields

Result grouping is a feature where results are clubbed together based on certain criteria. Solr provides us grouping based on field or based on queries. Let us search for all books and group results based on author name and genre. Grouping should be done on non-tokenized fields as the grouping output makes more sense for the complete field value rather than individual tokens. The non-tokenized string fields for author name and genre are `author_s` and `genre_s`. Why? Remember we discussed a concept known as dynamic fields in *Chapter 2, Inserting, Updating, and Deleting Documents from Solr*. The dynamic fields of type `*_s` is defined as `string` as shown in the following code, which is not tokenized in Solr:

```
<dynamicField name="*_s"  type="string"  indexed="true"
   stored="true" />
```

We will have to get the grouping component and add the fields we need to group by as shown in the following query:

```
$grp = $query->getGrouping();
$grp->addField('author_s');
$grp->addField('genre_s');
```

Let's also set the number of items that Solr should return for each group with the following query:

```
$grp->setLimit(3);
```

And also return the total number of groups with the following query:

```
$grp->setNumberOfGroups(true);
```

To display the grouping information we need to first get the grouping component from the result set with the following query:

```
$groups = $resultSet->getGrouping();
```

As we have done grouping on multiple fields we would be getting multiple groups in the result set. For each group in the groups array, we will get the number of matches and the number of group elements with the following code:

```
foreach($groups as $grpName => $grpFld)   {
echo '<h1> Grouped by ' . $grpName . '</h1>';
echo 'Total Matches: ' . $grpFld->getMatches();
echo 'Number of groups: ' . $grpFld->getNumberOfGroups();
foreach($grpFld as $grpVal)      {
echo '<h2>Grouping for ' . $grpVal->getValue() . ' : ' .
  $grpVal->getNumFound() . '</h2>';
foreach($grpVal as $doc){
echo $doc->id;
```

```
echo $doc->name;
echo $doc->author;
        }
    }
}
```

We are iterating over the number of group elements to find the name/heading and number of elements in the group. And for each group element get the documents from that group element.

The query in the Solr query logs is as follows:

```
1013311 [http-bio-8080-exec-2] INFO  org.apache.solr.core.SolrCore
  - [collection1] webapp=/solr path=/select
  params={omitHeader=true&group.ngroups=true&fl=id,name,
  author,series_t,score,last_modified&start=0&q=cat:book&group.
  limit=3&group.field=author_s&group.field=genre_s&
  group=true&wt=json&rows=25} hits=30 status=0 QTime=4
```

The parameters being passed are `group=true` to enable grouping and for each field we have a `group.field=<field_name>` parameter. The `group.limit` parameter is used to specify the number of documents to be retrieved for each group element. The output is as shown in the following screenshot:

Output of group by field.

Grouping results by queries

Instead of grouping by a field, we can also group by query. Let us create groups for different price ranges. Instead of using the addField() function on the grouping component, we have to use the addQuery() function and specify our query as a parameter in the function as shown in the following:

```
$grp->addQuery('price:[0 TO 5]');
$grp->addQuery('price:[5.01 TO 10]');
$grp->addQuery('price:[10.01 TO *]');
```

Here we have created 3 groups for price ranges $0 to $5, $5.01 to $10 and more than $10.

We can also set sorting within a group using the setSort() function as shown in the following query:

```
$grp->setSort('price desc');
```

Code to display the groups is similar to that discussed earlier. Output from our code is shown in the following screenshot:

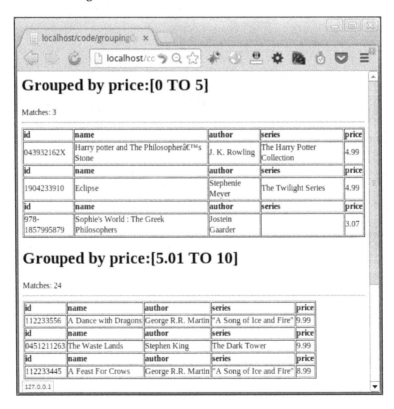

From Solr logs we can see that instead of `group.field` parameter we have got multiple `group.query` parameters.

```
1404903 [http-bio-8080-exec-4] INFO
  org.apache.solr.core.SolrCore  - [collection1] webapp=/solr
  path=/select params={omitHeader=true&group.ngroups=true&fl=id,
  name,author,series_t,score,price&start=0&q=cat:book
  &group.limit=3&group.query=price:[0+TO+5]&group.query=price:
  [5.01+TO+10]&group.query=price:[10.01+TO+*]
  &group.sort=price+desc&group=true&wt=json&rows=25} hits=30
  status=0 QTime=38
```

Running more like this query using PHP

More like this feature of Solr can be used to construct a query based on the terms within a document. This feature helps us in retrieving documents similar to those in our query results. We have to specify the fields on which the more like this functionality is run. For efficiency purposes, it is recommended that we have `termVectors=true` for these fields. Let us understand how this functionality works by looking at an example. Suppose we want books that are similar to those appearing in the result. Similarity of books is derived from the author and the series to which they belong. So we would have to tell Solr to get books similar to the currently selected book based on the fields' `author` and `series`. Solr (Lucene) internally compares all the tokens within the specified fields in all documents (books in our case) in the index with the fields of the currently selected book. And based on how many tokens are matching, it retrieves the results and ranks them so that the documents with maximum token matches are on top.

Let us add `termVectors=true` to our fields `author&*_t` (for `series_t`). Term vector is a collection of term frequency pairs optionally with positional information. Term vectors are basic building blocks for a Solr/Lucene index. We will need to index the documents again.

> For more information on how Lucene index works check out the documentation at `http://lucene.apache.org/core/4_5_1/core/org/apache/lucene/codecs/lucene45/package-summary.html`

In our PHP code, we will have to get the `MoreLikeThis` component from the query and add the fields on which we want to run this feature as shown in the following:

```
$mltquery = $query->getMoreLikeThis();
$mltquery->setFields('author,series_t');
```

This code says that we want to run the more like this similarity feature on fields' `author` and `series_t`. This should work for fairly large data sets but let's give it a few tweaks to make it run for our small books index using the following query:

```
$mltquery->setMinimumDocumentFrequency(1);
$mltquery->setMinimumTermFrequency(1);
```

This sets the minimum limits for classifying a document as a similar document. We will discuss more about these parameters in the 'tuning more like this query parameters' section.

After running the query, we need to get the more like this component from the result set. And then while processing the documents in the result set, we need to get the similar documents from the more like this `resultset` component as shown in the following code:

```
$resultset = $client->select($query);
$mltResult = $resultset->getMoreLikeThis();
foreach($resultset as $doc) {
echo $doc->id.', '.$doc->name.', '.$doc->author;
$mltdocs = $mltResult->getResult($doc->id);
if($mltdocs)    {
echo "\n".$mltdocs->getMaximumScore();
echo "\n".$mltdocs->getNumFound();
echo 'Docs fetched : '.count($mltdocs);
foreach($mltdocs as $mltdoc){
echo "\n".$mltdoc->id.' : '.$mltdoc->name.' ['.$mltdoc->score.']
    ';
        }
    }
}
```

Once we get the similar documents for a document, we can loop through the documents and get the details of similar documents. The following screenshot shows the output of this program:

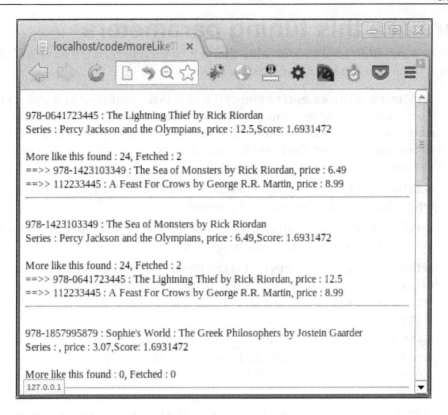

We can see in the Solr logs that the two main parameters that are passed to Solr are `mlt=true` & `mlt.fl=author,series_t`. To see the same result directly from Solr we can use the following query at `http://localhost:8080/solr/collection1/select/?mlt=true&rows=10&mlt.count=2&mlt.mindf=1&mlt.fl=author,series_t&fl=id,name,author,series_t,score,price&start=0&q=cat:book&mlt.mintf=1`.

Here the parameters are explained as follows:

- **mlt.count**: This specifies the number of similar documents that we want to fetch for each document in the result set
- **mlt.mindf**: This is the minimum document frequency at which words will be ignored which do not occur in at least these many documents
- **mlt.mintf**: This is the minimum term frequency after which terms will be ignored in the source document

More like this tuning parameters

Let us see some additional functionality that can be used to tune the more like this feature. We can use the following functions:

- **setMinimumDocumentFrequency()** and **setMinimumTermFrequency()**: These are to set the minimum document frequency and minimum term frequency that we saw earlier. If the variables are not set they are not passed to Solr and Solr uses the default parameters of `minimumDocumentFrequency` as 5 and `minimumTermFrequency` as 2.

- **setMinimumWordLength()**: This can be used to set the minimum word length below which words will be ignored.

- **setMaximumWordLength()**: This can be used to set the maximum word length above which words will be ignored.

- **setMaximumQueryTerms()**: This can be used to set the maximum number of query terms that will be included in any generated query. If it is not set it is not passed to Solr and in that case the default value of Solr which is 25 is applied.

- **setMaximumNumberOfTokens()**: This can be used to set the maximum number of tokens to parse in each doc field that is not stored with `TermVector` support. Default is 5000 which will be applied if we do not pass any parameter to Solr.

- **setBoost()**: If `true` it boosts the query by the interesting term relevance. Default is `false`.

- **setCount()**: This can be used to set the `mlt.count` parameter in Solr. It specifies how many similar documents to fetch for each document in the result set.

- **setQueryFields()**: This can be used to specify the query fields and their boosts. These fields must also be set in `setFields()` function.

Distributed search

When an index becomes too large to fit in a single machine, we can shard it and distribute it across multiple machines. Sharding requires a strategy that decides the shard to which a document is to be indexed based on certain values in certain fields. This strategy can be based on date, type of documents and so on. Though indexing has to happen separately for multiple shards, the search has to happen through a single interface. We should be able to specify the shards and the query should be run on all shards and return results for all shards. Solarium makes searching across multiple shards easy. Solarium supports distributed search through the

`DistributedSearch` component. This allows us to query multiple shards using a single interface and get results from all shards.

Another way of scaling your search infrastructure is to create a master-slave Solr architecture. Master can be used to add documents in your index and slaves can be used to provide search. This architecture can help scale the search over a large number of servers. It is generally recommended to create an infrastructure that has both replicas and shards. The Solr cloud is a solution that provides such an infrastructure with easy management and monitoring.

Setting up a distributed search

Let us create a new Solr instance that we will use as a separate shard. Go to the directory where Solr is installed and create a copy of the `example` folder, `example2`. This creates a new instance of Solr where the index and schema are copied. Now start the Solr server inside the `example2` folder. We have a new Solr instance running on port 8983. Our earlier instance is running on port 8080.

The corresponding commands for Linux users are:

```
cd <Solr home>
cp -r example example2
cd example2
java -jar start.jar -Djetty.port=8983
```

For Windows users, you can simply copy the `example` folder using Windows Explorer and then run `java-jar start.jar -Djetty.port=8983` in command prompt after `cd` to example2 folder.

To kill an existing server press *Ctrl* + *C* on your command prompt where the Solr server is running.

To check the Solr instance go to `http://localhost:8983/solr/`.

Since we have copied the index as well, the new instance of Solr will have all the documents that we had. Let us delete all the documents from the index and push some new documents to the index.

`http://localhost:8983/solr/update?stream.body=<delete><query>*:*</query></delete>`

`http://localhost:8983/solr/update?stream.body=<commit/>`

Add more books from the `books2.csv` file with the following command:

```
java -Durl=http://localhost:8983/solr/update -Dtype=application/csv
  -jar post.jar <path/to/file/>books2.csv
```

Executing a distributed search using PHP

To do a search on multiple shards, first we need to get the distributed search component from Solr. And then add shards to search as given in the following code:

```
$dSearch = $query->getDistributedSearch();
$dSearch->addShard('shard1','localhost:8080/solr');
$dSearch->addShard('shard2','localhost:8983/solr');
$resultSet = $client->select($query);
```

After executing the search we get a result set that has results from both the shards and can use it as we have used result sets earlier.

When we execute the search, we can see that Solr logs on both servers receive entries pertaining to this search. The parameters that are passed are `shard.url` (which contains the URL for Solr) and `isShard=true`.

Instead of adding shard one after another, we can add multiple shards in a single go using the `addShards()` function as given in the following:

```
$dSearch->addShards(array(
   'shard1' => 'localhost:8080/solr',
   'shard2' => 'localhost:8983/solr'
));
```

Solr has come out with the Solr cloud. So instead of using shards, we can set up a Solr cloud where data is automatically sharded and we can get in touch with any Solr instance to get the results of our query.

The Solr cloud has a concept of collections. So instead of adding cores, we will be required to add collections using the `addCollection()` or the `addCollections()` function. This functionality is available in Solarium 3.1 and higher.

Setting up Solr master-slave

We can set up Solr replication where the master Solr server is used for indexing and both master and slave Solr servers can be used for searches. Setting up replication is pretty simple in Solr. Check out the `requestHandler` named/`replication`. Simply create a copy of the `example` folder inside Solr as `example3` and empty the index files from the `example3` folder with the following command:

```
cp -r example example3
rm -rf example3/solr/collection1/data
```

In the master server (`example` folder), change the `solrconfig.xml` file to add configuration parameters for the replication master with the following code:

```
<lst name="master">
<str name="replicateAfter">commit</str>
<str name="replicateAfter">startup</str>
<str name="confFiles">schema.xml,stopwords.txt</str>
</lst>
```

Here, we have specified that replication should happen after a start up and after a commit on Solr. And the `schema.xml` and `stopwords.txt` files should be replicated.

On `slave` Solr (`example3` folder), change the `solrconfig.xml` file to add slave Solr configuration parameters. The parameters to be specified are the master Solr server URL and the poll interval for checking Solr. Here the poll interval is defined as HH:MM:SS (hours:minutes:seconds) as illustrated in the following code:

```
<lst name="slave">
<str name="masterUrl">http://localhost:8080/solr</str>
<str name="pollInterval">00:00:60</str>
</lst>
```

Restart Tomcat and start up the Solr server in `example3` folder using the `java -jar start.jar` command we have used earlier. This will start Solr on port 8983. This Solr server will act as the slave and poll the master for updates. All the index files are replicated on the slave Solr as shown in the following screenshot:

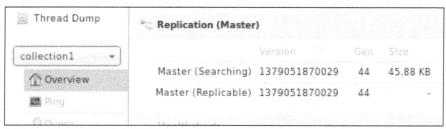

Solr interface for master server.

In the Solr interface for the master server as shown in the preceding screenshot, we can see that it is defined as the replication master with a version number for the index. In the Solr slave server as shown in the following, we can see that there is a slave and reference to master. Note that the version numbers are matching in the screenshot:

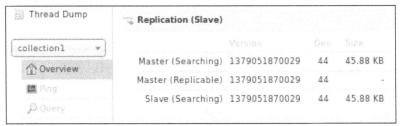

Solr interface for slave server.

Load balancing Solr queries using PHP

Solarium comes with a load balancer plugin that can be used to build redundancy among multiple Solr servers. The load balancer plugin has the following features:

- Support for multiple servers, each with their own weight.
- The ability to use a failover mode — try another Solr server if a query fails.
- Block certain query types. Updates are by default blocked.
- Force a specific server for the next query.

Add all Solr servers where you want to distribute your queries to your Solarium client configuration. In our case, we will be adding the master and slave Solr servers that we have recently set up with the following code:

```php
$config = array(
    "master" => array(
        "master" => array(
            "host"=>"127.0.0.1",
            "port"=>"8080",
            "path"=>"/solr",
            "core"=>"collection1",
        ),
    ),
    "slave" => array(
        "slave" => array(
            "host"=>"127.0.0.1",
            "port"=>"8983",
            "path"=>"/solr",
            "core"=>"collection1",
```

```
      ),
  )
);
```

Next, we need to create the endpoints from the Solarium client, get the load balancer plugin from the client and add the endpoints to the load balancer with respective weights as shown in the following code:

```
$masterEndpoint = $client->createEndpoint("master");
$slaveEndpoint = $client->createEndpoint("slave");
$lb = $client->getPlugin('loadbalancer');
$lb->addEndpoint($masterEndpoint, 1);
$lb->addEndpoint($slaveEndpoint, 5);
```

Enable failover to another Solr server after query fails on any server. Limit maximum number of retries to 2 before declaring the Solr server as unreachable and failing over to another server with the following queries:

```
$lb->setFailoverEnabled(true);
$lb->setFailoverMaxRetries(2);
```

Here we have set the weight of master server as 1 and slave server as 5. So on average 1 out of 6 queries will go to the master. If we want to force a query on the master, we can use the setForcedEndpointForNextQuery() function as shown in the following query:

```
$lb->setForcedEndpointForNextQuery('master');
```

Summary

In this chapter, we discussed some of the advanced functionalities available in Solr and the Solarium library. We saw grouping of results based on field and query. And we also saw a functionality known as more like this, which can be used to extract results similar to a particular document from Solr based on some fields of the original document. We saw how to scale Solr beyond a single machine using replication and sharding. And we saw the functionalities provided by Solarium for scaling Solr.

Index

N

name attribute 23
name variable 76

P

PeclHttp adapter 20
PHP
  used, for adding documents to Solr 27, 28
  used, for deleting documents in Solr 30, 31
  used, for executing distributed search 94
  used, for executing ping query on Solr 11-18
  used, for highlighting in Solr 59, 60
  used, for implementing autocomplete feature 81-83
  used, for load balancing Solr queries 96, 97
  used, for running more like this query 89-91
  used, for running spell check 78-80
  used, for updating documents to Solr 28, 29
PHP-Solr integration 13, 14
ping query
  executing on Solr, PHP used 11-17
  executing on Solr, Solarium library used 17
pivot
  facet by 54, 55
positionIncrementGap attribute 22
precisionStep attribute 22
pspell 75

Q

query
  alternatives 44
  executing, DisMax used 40-42
  executing, eDisMax used 40-42
  facet by 51, 52
  results, grouping by 88, 89
  re-using 36-38
  running, select configuration used 36
  select query creating, return fields used 34, 35
  select query creating, sorting used 34, 35
queryNorm 66

R

range
  facet by 53, 54
regular highlighter 57
removeField($fieldStr) function 36
removeSort($sortStr) function 36
required attribute 23
results
  grouping, by field 86, 87
  grouping, by query 88, 89
RESULTSPERPAGE 37

S

schema.xml file 22
select configuration
  used, for running query 36
select query
  creating, return fields used 34, 35
  creating, sorting used 34, 35
setAlternateField(string $field) function 63
setAuthentication(string $username, string $password) setting 19
setBoost() function 92
setBoostFunctions() function 41
setBoostFunctionsMult() function 41, 42
setCollateExtendedResults() function 79
setCount() function 92
setDefaultEndpoint(string $endpoint) setting 19
setExtendedResults() function 79
setLimit(int $limit) function 49
setMaxAlternateFieldLength(int $length) function 63
setMaximumNumberOfTokens() function 92
setMaximumQueryTerms() function 92
setMaximumWordLength() function 92
setMinimumDocumentFrequency() function 92
setMinimumTermFrequency() function 92
setMinimumWordLength() function 92
setOffset(int $offset) function 49
setPhraseBigramFields() function 41
setPhraseBigramSlop() function 41

W

Z

Thank you for buying
Apache Solr PHP Integration

About Packt Publishing

Packt, pronounced 'packed', published its first book "*Mastering phpMyAdmin for Effective MySQL Management*" in April 2004 and subsequently continued to specialize in publishing highly focused books on specific technologies and solutions.

Our books and publications share the experiences of your fellow IT professionals in adapting and customizing today's systems, applications, and frameworks. Our solution based books give you the knowledge and power to customize the software and technologies you're using to get the job done. Packt books are more specific and less general than the IT books you have seen in the past. Our unique business model allows us to bring you more focused information, giving you more of what you need to know, and less of what you don't.

Packt is a modern, yet unique publishing company, which focuses on producing quality, cutting-edge books for communities of developers, administrators, and newbies alike. For more information, please visit our website: www.packtpub.com.

About Packt Open Source

In 2010, Packt launched two new brands, Packt Open Source and Packt Enterprise, in order to continue its focus on specialization. This book is part of the Packt Open Source brand, home to books published on software built around Open Source licences, and offering information to anybody from advanced developers to budding web designers. The Open Source brand also runs Packt's Open Source Royalty Scheme, by which Packt gives a royalty to each Open Source project about whose software a book is sold.

Writing for Packt

We welcome all inquiries from people who are interested in authoring. Book proposals should be sent to author@packtpub.com. If your book idea is still at an early stage and you would like to discuss it first before writing a formal book proposal, contact us; one of our commissioning editors will get in touch with you.

We're not just looking for published authors; if you have strong technical skills but no writing experience, our experienced editors can help you develop a writing career, or simply get some additional reward for your expertise.

Administrating Solr

ISBN: 978-1-78328-325-5   Paperback: 120 pages

Master the use of Drupal and associated scripts to administrate, monitor, and optimize Solr

1. Learn how to work with monitoring tools like OpsView, New Relic, and SPM

2. Utilize Solr scripts and Collection Distribution scripts to manage Solr

3. Employ search features like querying, categorizing, search based on location, and distributed search

Scaling Big Data with Hadoop and Solr

ISBN: 978-1-78328-137-4   Paperback: 144 pages

Learn exciting new ways to build efficient, high performance enterprise search repositories for Big Data using Hadoop and Solr

1. Understand the different approaches of making Solr work on Big Data as well as the benefits and drawbacks

2. Learn from interesting, real-life use cases for Big Data search along with sample code

3. Work with the Distributed Enterprise Search without prior knowledge of Hadoop and Solr

Please check **www.PacktPub.com** for information on our titles

Apache Solr 4 Cookbook

ISBN: 978-1-78216-132-5   Paperback: 328 pages

Over 100 recipes to make Apache Solr faster, more reliable, and return better results

1. Learn how to make Apache Solr search faster, more complete, and comprehensively scalable

2. Solve performance, setup, configuration, analysis, and query problems in no time

3. Get to grips with, and master, the new exciting features of Apache Solr 4

Learning FuelPHP for Effective PHP Development

ISBN: 978-1-78216-036-6   Paperback: 108 pages

Use the flexible FuelPHP framework to quickly and effectively create PHP applications

1. Scaffold with oil - the FuelPHP command-line tool

2. Build an administration quickly and effectively

3. Create your own project using FuelPHP

Please check **www.PacktPub.com** for information on our titles